The War of the Worlds

H.G. WELLS

WORKBOOK

Notes and activities: Jane Branson
Series consultant: Peter Buckroyd

OXFORD
UNIVERSITY PRESS

Contents

What are Oxford Literature Companions?

Oxford Literature Companions is a series designed to provide you with comprehensive support for popular set texts. You can use the Companion workbook alongside your novel, using relevant sections during your studies or using the workbook as a whole for revision. The workbook will help you to create your own personalized guide to the text.

What are the main features within this workbook?

Each workbook in the Oxford Literature Companion series follows the same approach and includes the following features:

Activities

Each workbook offers a range of varied and in-depth activities to deepen understanding and encourage close work with the text, covering characters, themes, language and context. The Skills and Practice chapter also offers advice on assessment and includes sample questions and student answers. There are spaces to write your answers throughout the workbook.

Key terms and quotations

Throughout the workbook, key terms are highlighted in the text and explained on the same page. There is also a detailed glossary at the end of the workbook that explains, in the context of the novel, all the relevant literary terms highlighted.

Quotations from the novel appear in blue text throughout this workbook.

Upgrade

As well as providing guidance on key areas of the novel, throughout this workbook you will also find 'Upgrade' features. These are tips to help with your exam preparation and performance.

Progress check

Each chapter of the workbook ends with a 'Progress check'. Through self-assessment, these enable you to establish how confident you feel about what you have been learning and help you to set next steps and targets.

Which edition of the novel has this workbook used?

Quotations have been taken from the Oxford University Press edition of *The War of the Worlds* (ISBN: 978-019-839624-6)

Plot and Structure

Understanding plot

Although you are reading *The War of the Worlds* because you are going to be examined on it, it is important to think about how and why Wells set out to write this story. Ideally, read the whole book all the way through for enjoyment and then start rereading for study purposes.

> **plot** the main events of a play, novel, film, or similar work, presented by the writer as an interrelated sequence

Activity 1

Keep a reading log. Start your reading log below and continue on separate paper. Add a few lines of notes every time you read, to keep track of main events of the **plot** as well as your feelings and reactions. Here is an example to get you started:

Pages read	What is happening?	My thoughts and feelings
Beginning of Chapter 1	In Chapter 1, the narrator reflects – a bit vaguely – on events that took place in the past, 'The storm burst upon us six years ago now', and talks about Mars as if we share his knowledge. He describes a night in an observatory when he saw missiles being launched from Mars – though he didn't know they were missiles at the time, 'It seemed so safe and tranquil.'	I don't really know who the narrator is. He seems a bit of a show-off, putting forward theories about the Martians and comparing them to the people on Earth who have 'infinite complacency'. There's a sense of impending doom.

Upgrade

Notice that this student is already beginning to incorporate short quotations into their notes. You should do this too – it will help you to become more familiar with the text. Knowing a number of short quotations from throughout the novel will help you to feel confident in the exam and you will be able to embed them easily in your written answers.

Sequencing and summarizing

Keeping track of the action is important: by the time you get to the exam, you will need to have strong recall of all the major scenes and events in the story.

Activity 2

a) Listed below are some of the main events in the novel, but they are in the wrong order. Number the events 1 to 12 to show the sequence in which they are recounted in the novel.

The narrator meets the curate.

The astronomer Ogilvy invites the narrator to the observatory to see the lights on Mars.

The narrator avoids a Heat-Ray attack by diving into the river.

Fire breaks out on Horsell Common.

Dead Martians are found in a pit.

The narrator discovers how the Martians consume the blood from still-living animals.

There is a battle between Martians and a warship off the Essex coast.

The first Martian emerges out of its cylinder.

The narrator helps the artilleryman with his tunnel digging.

The narrator leaves his wife in Leatherhead.

The narrator is reunited with his wife.

A Martian drags the curate away.

b) Which of the events listed above take place in the narrator's brother's part of the story?

c) Develop your knowledge of this part of the text by writing your own list of key events that take place within the narrator's brother's part of the story.

The events in this novel are not always recounted in **chronological** order. For example, the main events happened six years before the narration begins and the episodes featuring the narrator's brother take place in a different time sequence altogether. As well as making sure you know the events in the order they are recounted (See Activities 1 and 2), you should be able to organize them into chronological order. The main events in the novel take place over four weeks.

chronological in the order in which events occur

Activity 3

Consolidate your understanding of the weekly events by writing a series of short, factual diary entries in the voice of the narrator, one for each week and recording only what the narrator knows. See below for an example of how to begin the first entry. If needed, continue on a separate sheet of paper.

Week 1

Earth is being attacked by invaders from Mars. I have seen one of them up close and witnessed its ability to kill by shooting fire and...

Week 2

Week 3

Week 4

Activity 4

Now work further on your ability to recall the whole plot. Think carefully about what you need to focus on and leave out. This will help you to reflect on the key episodes.

a) Write the entire plot in ten bullet points.

b) Summarize the novel in four sentences.

Setting

Having a strong visual sense of the **setting** and the narrator's movements is a good way to help you remember the sequence of events, and also reveal some important aspects of the book's structure.

> **setting** the physical and geographical backdrop of a play, novel, film, or similar work

Activity 5

Use this map of the relevant area to highlight the key places in the narrator's journey. Annotate his journey line and stop-off points with:

- notes about the events in each place or on each stage of the journey
- the names of characters the narrator encounters in each place
- short quotations which sum up the key events in each place.

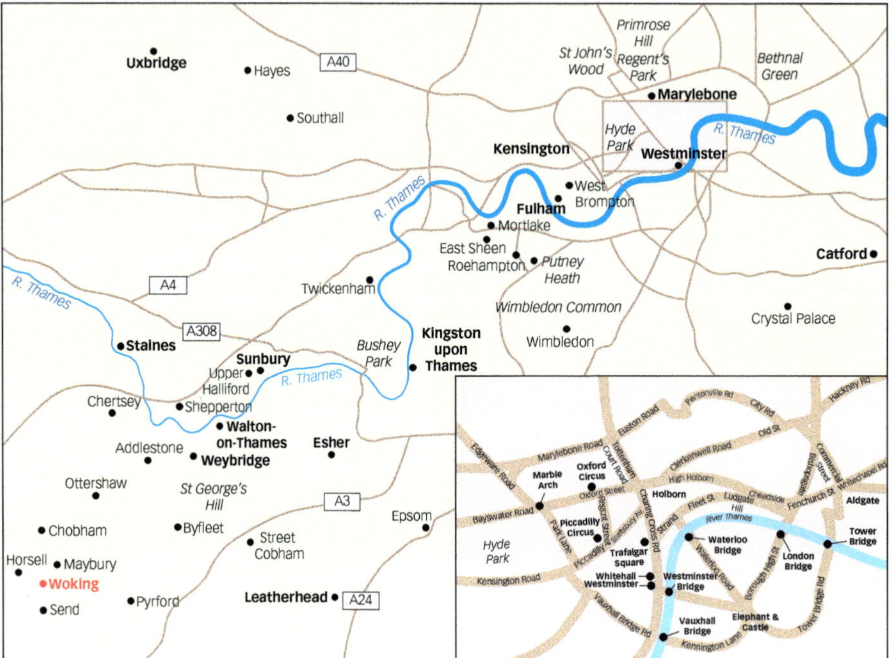

Activity 6

a) The places mentioned in the book are real places where people still live today. Why do you think Wells chose a realistic setting?

----

b) Why do you think Wells wanted the narrator to revisit some places and end up in the same place as he started?

Understanding structure

Tracking patterns in a text is another good way to understand how its plot works and draws your attention to **structure** too.

structure the way a text develops across its parts

Activity 7

a) Track Wells's creation of tension through Book 1 of the novel by completing the table below. Reread the final paragraphs of each chapter, and decide how tense or dramatic things are at these points.

    i. Rate the tension with a score out of 10 and give brief reasons for your thinking, as in the example.

    ii. Note a short quotation that you feel is relevant to the level of tension.

Book and chapter	Key quotation	Tension score	Reasons
Book 1			
1	**'It seemed so safe and tranquil.'**	6	Contrast with the chapter title and the events referred to creates tension
2			
3			
4			
5			
6			
7			
8			
9			
10			
11			
12			
13			
14			
15			
16			
17			

b) Transfer your tension evaluations on to a graph. The line you draw to connect all the plot points will be an indication of where tension is high and whether the drama rises or falls across Book 1.

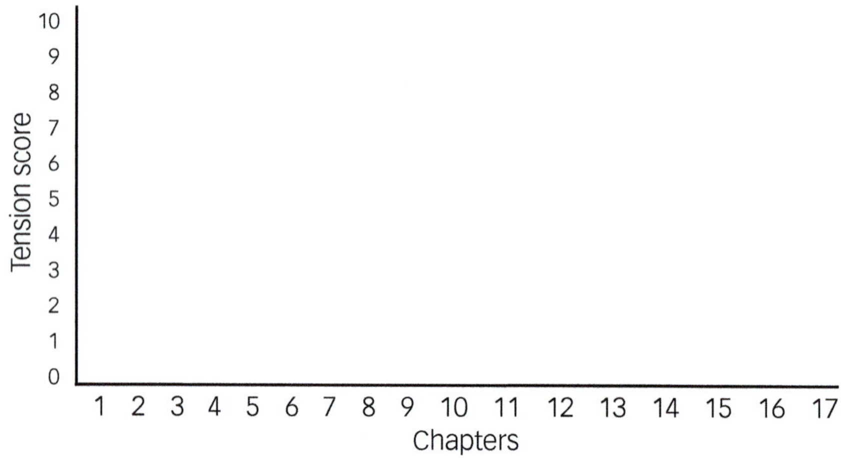

c) Select two key moments of higher tension and two moments of lower tension. Make notes about the effect on the reader at each moment and why you think Wells wanted the tension to be high and low at these points.

----

d) Scan through Book 2 of the novel and select two points of high tension or drama, then complete the table below.

Chapter	Summary of dramatic event	Key quotation	What creates the drama or tension at this point?

Another pattern to track across *The War of the Worlds* is the way Wells builds up the reader's image of the Martians. Their appearance, behaviour and impact are all gradually developed, reflecting the narrator's growing understanding of them and the way they affect his world.

Activity 8

Trace the way Wells develops his picture of the Martians, using the table below. Select relevant details and quotations from the chapters indicated, and note the narrator's reactions.

Reference	Details and quotations	The narrator's reaction and understanding of the Martians
Book 1, Chapter 3 First description of the Martians	**'unusual shape and colour'** **'the ashy incrustation'**	The narrator reports without comment on Ogilvy's descriptions. There is a focus on facts and scientific description rather than feelings.
Book 1, Chapters 3, 4 Further detail about the Martians' appearance		
Book 1, Chapter 5 How the Martians kill		
Book 1, Chapters 10, 11 How the Martians move		
Book 1, Chapter 12 The Martians in battle		
Book 1, Chapter 15 How the Martians sound, their technology and weapons		
Book 1, Chapter 17 Description of the coastal battle		
Book 2, Chapter 1 Martians pursuing and capturing humans		
Book 2, Chapters 2, 3, 4 Martian behaviour and technology		
Book 2, Chapter 8 Description of the dead Martians		

It is important to look at the text as a whole to understand how it is structured and its key turning points. The following aspects of the text can all be seen as structural decisions:

- Where the story begins – what is happening as the author drops us into the story
- Shifts in location
- When the mood or atmosphere changes
- When the point of view or narrative perspective changes
- Flashbacks or foregrounding moments
- What the author chooses to put in the middle of the story
- Skipping over longer sequences of time
- Dwelling on very short periods of time
- Periods of action, dialogue, description or reflection
- Particularly short or long chapters
- How the author ends the story

Watch out for these changes and turning points in your reading. They often indicate that the author is playing with structure, and your reading will be strengthened if you think about why. The following activity will also help with this.

Activity 9

Review the following statements to help you think about what kind of story this is, judging each one as 'true' or 'false' *in your opinion*.

Statements	True	False
The novel has a simple beginning–middle–end structure.		
The story contains a number of viewpoints and stories within stories.		
The novel is the story of one person, but it's also a story about the human race.		
There is no tension in the story because we know from the beginning that the narrator survives.		
The plot is a classic one consisting of a situation that gets complicated or tense and then, after a climax in the action, things are resolved.		

Overcoming the monster

One way of reading *The War of the Worlds* is as an **overcoming the monster tale**, like the traditional stories of *Beowulf* and *Little Red Riding Hood*, the Greek myth of *Theseus* or *Jaws* (book by Peter Benchley, film by Steven Spielberg).

overcoming the monster tale one of the plot types identified by Christopher Booker in his book *The Seven Basic Plots*, in which he explains his theory that all stories match one of seven plots with predictable features and character types

Activity 10

This table shows the five main stages of an 'overcoming the monster' narrative. Use the second column to add bullet points to consider whether *The War of the Worlds* matches up to this type of plot structure or not.

Stage of the story	How *The War of the Worlds* matches up
Anticipation: The reader finds out about the monster. There is tension and a 'call for action' for the hero.	
Dream: The hero gets ready to fight the monster. It looks as though things will be all right.	
Frustration: The monster arrives and its power is revealed. Things look bad for the hero.	
Nightmare: Things go from bad to worse for the hero until…	
Escape: The monster is overcome by the hero, who may have extra help or new information. There is a happy ending for the reader.	

Writing about plot and structure

To understand a plot fully, it is important to notice small details as well as major episodes or events. Examiners will expect you to be able to comment on the significance of events, what they symbolize and what layers of meaning they create in the text.

The characteristics of some strong and weaker responses to questions about plot are shown in the table below.

Strong answers	Weak answers
Main events of plot referred to and important details picked out.	Shows knowledge of some of the main events.
Range of comments about how plot links to other aspects of the novel, such as character development and atmosphere.	Limited comments about how plot links to other aspects of the novel, such as character development and atmosphere.
Students focus on what the events mean or suggest, using expressions such as 'hints at', 'underlines', 'emphasizes' and 'making the reader wonder' to explore less obvious meanings.	Students just retell the story using their own words.

Activity 11

a) Read the exam question and the extract below. Then read the two student responses.

b) Use the table about weak and strong answers to help you annotate the two answers as if you are the teacher, explaining the strengths and weaknesses of each, and giving advice on improvements if they are needed.

> How does Wells use events in this extract to create atmosphere?

Saturday lives in my memory as a day of suspense. It was a day of lassitude[1] too, hot and close, with, I am told, a rapidly fluctuating barometer[2]. I had slept but little, though my wife had succeeded in sleeping, and I rose early. I went into my garden before breakfast and stood listening, but towards the common there was nothing stirring but a lark.

The milkman came as usual. I heard the rattle of his chariot and I went round to the side gate to ask the latest news. He told me that during the night the Martians had been surrounded by troops, and that guns were expected. Then – a familiar, reassuring note – I heard a train running towards Woking.

'They aren't to be killed,' said the milkman, 'if that can possibly be avoided.'

I saw my neighbour gardening, chatted with him for a time, and then strolled in to breakfast. It was a most unexceptional morning. My neighbour was of the opinion that the troops would be able to capture or to destroy the Martians during the day.

'It's a pity they make themselves so unapproachable,' he said. 'It would be curious to know how they live on another planet; we might learn a thing or two.'

He came up to the fence and extended a handful of strawberries, for his gardening was as generous as it was enthusiastic. At the same time, he told me of the burning of the pine-woods about the Byfleet Gold Links[3]. (*Book 1, Chapter 9*)

1 lassitude – physical or mental weariness

2 barometer – an instrument for measuring atmospheric pressure

3 Byfleet Gold Links – a golf course

Student A

The narrator tells the reader about his Saturday morning, which involves breakfast, walking in the garden and chatting to the neighbour. There isn't much of a dramatic atmosphere because the narrator seems quite relaxed, not tense. He enjoys hearing the train go by because it means things are ordinary. The milkman comes and the neighbour gives him some strawberries. Everything seems to be normal.

Student B

The narrator's comments about the 'fluctuating barometer', the 'hot and close' weather and his lack of sleep add up to a feeling of anxiety, but generally the events recounted in the passage are 'as usual', including the milkman's visit and the neighbour's gift of some strawberries. This suggests people are trying to carry on normally in new and terrifying conditions, which creates an underlying tension. The different views about the Martians – that they are 'surrounded by troops', 'not to be killed' and 'so unapproachable' – suggest that no one really knows what is happening. These words also contrast with other, 'unexceptional' sounds, such as the lark and the train, which adds further to the atmosphere of mystery and doom.

Now read the extract below, thinking carefully about what the author is intending to convey to the reader.

> About five o'clock the gathering crowd in the station was immensely excited by the opening of the line of communication, which is almost invariably closed, between the South-Eastern and the South-Western stations, and the passage of carriage trucks bearing huge guns and carriages crammed with soldiers. These were the guns that were brought up from Woolwich and Chatham to cover Kingston. There was an exchange of pleasantries: 'You'll get eaten!' 'We're the beast-tamers!' and so forth. A little while after that a squad of police came into the station and began to clear the public off the platforms, and my brother went out into the street again.
>
> The church bells were ringing for evensong, and a squad of Salvation Army lassies came singing down Waterloo Road. On the bridge a number of loafers were watching a curious brown scum that came drifting down the stream in patches. The sun was just setting, and the Clock Tower and the Houses of Parliament rose against one of the most peaceful skies it is possible to imagine, a sky of gold, barred with long transverse stripes of reddish-purple cloud. There was talk of a floating body. One of the men there, a reservist he said he was, told my brother he had seen the heliograph* flickering in the west. (*Book 1, Chapter 14*)
>
> * heliograph – a sun-reflecting signalling device

Activity 12

Practise commenting on the significance of plot and events by answering the following questions:

a) What is the public attitude to the arrival of soldiers?

----

b) The narrator, or his brother, have various patronizing names for 'ordinary people', including **'lassies'** and **'loafers'**. Why do you think they use these terms?

----

c) What is the importance of the **'brown scum'** that is seen on the water?

----

d) Why is the mention of **'the heliograph'** significant?

Activity 13

Now try writing about plot and structure again. This time, do it without prompts and choose your own extract to comment on. For example, you could select the narrator's return home after the first Heat-Ray attack (Book 1, Chapter 7) or the attack of the *Thunder Child* on the Martians (Book 1, Chapter 17).

Whichever extract you choose, answer this question:

'Write about the significance of the events in the passage and the way that Wells presents them.'

Activity 14

a) Read back over what you have written in Activity 13 and reflect on the following questions:

    i. Have you done more than tell the story?

    ii. Have you suggested what actions and events might mean?

    iii. Have you suggested less obvious layers of meaning?

b) If necessary, make changes to your response to improve it. You may need to redraft it on separate paper.

Foreshadowing

One of the structural features that Wells uses effectively in *The War of the Worlds* is called **foreshadowing**. This device draws attention to important themes, helps to build tension and to create ominous clues about future events.

> **foreshadowing** when an author gives clues, warnings and indications about future events

Activity 15

Complete the table below to show which events (from early in the novel) foreshadow other, later events. You may need to include more than one event in the first column, as in the example that has been completed.

Early events that foreshadow...	... later events
The report of Ogilvy's realization that **'something within the cylinder was unscrewing the top!'** (*Book 1, Chapter 2*) The slow unscrewing of the cylinder as observed by the narrator (*Book 1, Chapter 4*).	The emergence of the Martian from its cylinder when it finally opens (*Book 1, Chapter 4*).
	The death of the curate (*Book 2, Chapter 4*).
	The narrator sees the Martians **'dead! – slain by the putrefactive and disease bacteria against which their systems were unprepared'** (*Book 2, Chapter 8*).
	The narrator's reunion with his wife (*Book 2, Chapter 9*).
	The narrator's fragile mental state: **'an abiding sense of doubt and insecurity'** (*Book 2, Chapter 10*).

Key quotation

A question of graver and universal interest is the possibility of another attack from the Martians. I do not think that nearly enough attention is being given to this aspect of the matter... (*Book 2, Chapter 10*)

Remember that when you are writing about the plot of the text, you will limit your marks if you just give a simple recounting of events. Instead, you need to think carefully about how and why the author has constructed and presented events in a particular way and order, narrated by a particular character and with what particular effect on the reader.

Upgrade

Progress check

Use the chart below to review the skills you have developed in this chapter. For each column, start at the bottom box and work your way up towards the highest level in the top box. Tick the box to show you have achieved that level.

Personal response	Language, structure, form
I can sustain a critical response to *The War of the Worlds* and interpret the plot and structure convincingly	I can analyse the effects of Wells's use of language, structure and form in *The War of the Worlds*, using subject terms judiciously
I can develop a coherent response to *The War of the Worlds* and explain the plot and structure clearly	I can explain how Wells uses language, structure and form to create effects in *The War of the Worlds*, using relevant subject terms
I can make some comments on the plot and structure in *The War of the Worlds*	I can identify some of Wells's methods in *The War of the Worlds* and use some subject terms

Context

Understanding context

The **context** of any piece of art can be taken into account to help understand it. In literature, context might include any of the following:

* when a text was written

* events that were happening around the time the text was written and how these may have influenced the writing

* the life experiences of the author and how they are relevant to the writing

* other works of literature and art produced at the same time or about similar themes or topics and how these may have influenced the text

* the ideas that were commonly believed at the time the text was written and how these are relevant to it.

> **Key quotation**
>
> **The most extraordinary thing to my mind, of all the strange and wonderful things that happened upon that Friday, was the dovetailing of the commonplace habits of our social order with the first beginnings of the series of events that was to topple that social order headlong.**
> *(Book 1, Chapter 8)*

You must avoid just filling your exam responses with facts about Wells's life and influences. To gain marks, you need to explain how the context of the novel influenced its writing, and its effect on readers.

Activity 1

Complete the table below by filling the second column with notes about how each aspect of context might link to the text.

Facts about context	Link to the text
Some of H.G. Wells's life (1866–1946) was spent as a Victorian, a period when the idea of evolution was of great interest and Charles Darwin put forward his theory of **natural selection**.	Wells explores the idea of evolution in several ways. The Martians, for example, are his vision of how life has evolved on another planet. Also, in Book 2, Chapter 7, the artilleryman voices the idea that certain people, who have adapted well, will survive the invasion.
Wells's life and times were affected by the legacy of the **Industrial Revolution**, which impacted on people's experience of machines, work and travel.	

Like many novels at the time, *The War of the Worlds* was first published as a **serial** in a magazine in 1897. (Hint: Think about the chapter episodes, chapter lengths and chapter endings.)	
Nowadays, Wells is often called 'the father of **science fiction**'. *The War of the Worlds* followed in the footsteps of several early books about Mars and Martians, as well as titles such as *Journey to the Centre of the Earth* by Jules Verne.	
Politically, Wells was a **socialist**, influenced by his own experiences of coming from a working-class family who often endured poverty.	

Industrial Revolution the introduction of machinery into Britain in the late 18th and early 19th centuries. The period was characterized by the use of steam power, the growth of factories, and the mass production of manufactured goods

natural selection Charles Darwin's theory that weaker and less able creatures die out over time, leaving stronger, more able species to survive

science fiction fiction based on imagined future scientific or technological advances and major social or environmental changes, frequently portraying space or time travel and life on other planets

serial a story or play appearing in regular instalments, for example in a magazine. In Victorian times, this was a popular way of publishing stories in a more affordable format at a time when few could afford to buy books

socialist a political view that property, business and possessions should be owned and run by the community for everyone's benefit

Activity 2

Wells explores a range of other ideas in the novel. As an introduction to these ideas, research the topics in the first column of the following table, using the middle column to record what you discover and how you think the ideas link to *The War of the Worlds*.

Topic	What does this mean and what is its relevance to *The War of the Worlds*?	Relevant quotations from the text
Eugenics		
The British Empire		
Horror fiction		
Fin de siècle		
The rise of technology		

Activity 3

a) Read the quotations below and decide which of the ideas in the Activity 2 table they best represent. Insert the quotations (or extracts from them) into the correct places on the table.

> "And we form a band – able-bodied, clean-minded men. We're not going to pick up any rubbish that drifts in. Weaklings go out again."
> *(Book 2, Chapter 7)*

> 'It was the beginning of the rout of civilization, of the massacre of mankind.'
> *(Book 1, Chapter 17)*

> '… before we judge of them too harshly we must remember what ruthless and utter destruction our own species has wrought, not only upon animals, such as the vanished bison and the dodo, but upon its inferior races.'
> *(Book 1, Chapter 1)*

> '… it was no mere insensate machine driving on its way. Machine it was, with a ringing metallic pace, and long, flexible, glittering tentacles…'
> *(Book 1, Chapter 10)*

> 'One of its gripping limbs curled amid the debris; another limb appeared, feeling its way over the fallen beams. I stood petrified, staring. Then I saw through a sort of glass plate near the edge of the body the face, as we may call it, and the large dark eyes of a Martian, peering, and then a long metallic snake of tentacle came feeling slowly through the hole.'
> *(Book 2, Chapter 4)*

b) Now locate your own quotations to supplement the ones that have been provided for you. Flicking through the text to hunt for relevant parts and selecting quotations is a useful activity that will improve your familiarity with the novel.

Short quotations of just a word or phrase can be just as effective as long quotations, particularly if they are embedded neatly into a sentence. For example:

The artilleryman voices the idea that men who are 'rubbish' or 'weaklings' will not survive in the new, post-invasion world.

At the time Wells was writing, the Empire's 'ruthless and utter destruction' and colonialization of other countries was very recent.

Religion

The War of the Worlds also explores ideas about religion. At the time of the novel's publication, Christianity was the main religion in Britain, with a range of denominations – such as Methodists, Baptists and Quakers – rising up alongside the dominant Anglican Church. During the Victorian era, many new churches were built and there was a large increase in the number of clergymen.

However, an increasing number of prominent people were beginning to voice doubts about religion and declare a lack of faith. In 1888, a law was passed allowing people of non-Christian backgrounds and atheists to serve as Members of Parliament. Wells took the view that although he believed in a 'personal and intimate God' (*God the Invisible King*, H.G. Wells, 1917), he did not see himself as a Christian.

Read the following extract from one student's work, written in response to a question about how religion is presented in *The War of the Worlds*.

Wells puts forward a range of views about God and religion that represent the time in which he was writing. For example, the curate sees the Martians as 'God's ministers', which contrasts with the narrator's scientific view of the invasion based on his first sight of it 'through a powerful telescope on earth'. Furthermore, H.G. Wells seems to be voicing some of the doubts about religion that he and other Victorians felt. When the curate speaks about the Martian attack as evidence of mankind being punished for its 'folly' and sin, the narrator dismisses him as full of 'weakness and insanity'. This is very different from the narrator's own praying, which he says he does 'steadfastly and sanely'. Like the curate, the artilleryman doesn't represent a positive picture of religion. He says it is what happens when 'a lot of people feel they ought to be doing something', which could be seen as Wells questioning the value of religion as science was beginning to do at the time he was writing.

Activity 4

Decide which of the teacher comments below go with which parts of the student's answer.

Highlight relevant text in the student's response and indicate the appropriate teacher comment by marking it with a number from 1 to 5. Note that some teacher comments are relevant to more than one part of the student's response.

1 Good reference to Wells's life and times as a Victorian.

2 Strong use of words and phrases to link points together.

3 Good use of embedded quotations from across the text.

4 Insightful comparisons between characters.

5 Thoughtful comments on religious ideas in the novel

Technological context

The Victorian era, which Wells was born into, saw the development of a wide range of inventions. Although many of them were relatively low-tech, the impact on life was wide-ranging. In the following activities, you will consider Wells's views of science and technology based on his life and times.

Activity 5

Research the year of invention of each of the following, and write them below. All the dates are in the 19th century! Wells focuses on some of these inventions in his writing.

Bicycle		Postage stamps	
Light bulbs		Photography	
Underground trains		X-rays	

Wells is also famous for 'predicting the future' of technology because he wrote about things that later became reality. For example, in his novel *The Island of Dr Moreau* (1896) he reveals the possibility of genetic engineering. And in *The War of the Worlds*, space travel and biological warfare are key to the story, though neither was a reality at the time Wells was writing.

Activity 6

Locate the technological aspects of the novel listed in the table below. Read the relevant section of the text and complete the task for each in the box provided.

Technological aspect	Task
Explanation of Mars (Book 1, Chapter 1)	Select three precise, scientific phrases that Wells uses to give the narrator scientific credibility.
The Heat-Ray (Book 1, Chapter 5)	List of three words or phrases that highlight the narrator's shock when the Martians deploy the Heat-Ray.
Description of the Martians (Book 2, Chapter 2)	Identify three ways in which Martians are different from humans.

Key quotation

For my own part, I was much occupied in learning to ride the bicycle, and busy upon a series of papers discussing the probable developments of moral ideas as civilization progressed.
(Book 1, Chapter 1)

Literary context

Another important aspect of the context of the novel comes from its literary connections. In writing *The War of the Worlds*, Wells drew upon well-established literary **genres**.

- The novel adopts the form of **fictional autobiography.**
- It is an early example of a science-fiction story or **scientific romance**.
- It is a story constructed around a journey, both real (around London) and metaphorical (because the narrator learns something about himself).
- It has elements of the horror and adventure genres.

fictional autobiography a fictional narrative written as though it is a true life story from a first-person point of view

genre a style or category of art, music, or literature

scientific romance a tale combining science and mysterious or imaginary elements

Activity 7

Insert ticks in the columns below to show which features of the novel link with the genres associated with the novel. Some features may be linked to more than one genre, as in the example that has been completed for you.

Feature of the novel	Fictional autobiography	Scientific romance	Journey story	Horror/ adventure
The narrator lives in a place that actually exists and refers continually to other real places in and near London.	✓		✓	
The story is about invaders from another planet.				
The narrator is a writer.				
The book contains some vivid depictions of death and destruction.				
The book follows the narrator as he travels around.				
The narrator has a range of experiences and has changed by the end of the novel.				
There are many descriptions of futuristic technology.				
The Martians are monsters and the descriptions of them are designed to shock or scare the reader.				
The book is written in the first person.				

Activity 8

a) Decide which quotations from the novel, below, link with the four literary genres mentioned on page 26. Copy them into the table below alongside the most appropriate genre.

b) Find your own quotations from the novel to add to this table.

> 'Once, even, it touched the heel of my boot. I was on the verge of screaming; I bit my hand. For a time the tentacle was silent.'
> *(Book 2, Chapter 4)*

> 'We can never anticipate the unseen good or evil that may come upon us suddenly out of space.'
> *(Book 2, Chapter 10)*

> '… I felt a wave of emotion that was near akin to tears.'
> *(Book 2, Chapter 8)*

> 'I saw an abandoned boat, very small and remote, drifting downstream; and throwing off the most of my sodden clothes, I went after it, gained it, and so escaped out of that destruction.'
> *(Book 1, Chapter 13)*

Genres	Quotations
Fictional autobiography	
Scientific romance	
Journey story	
Horror/adventure	

Upgrade

Research H.G. Wells's other novels, such as *The Invisible Man* and *The Time Machine*. You may not have time to read all of them but at least read the opening chapters and find out what they are about by looking up a synopsis of each. You may be able to use some of this information to make brief knowledgeable comparisons with *The War of the Worlds* in your exam response (if it is relevant to the question).

Developing your understanding of context

Showing a developed understanding of context in your writing about the novel means linking Wells's authorial choices to the context of his writing. The following activity will help you to do this.

> **fin de siècle** a French term (meaning 'end of the century') associated with the way that art and culture reflected changes happening at the end of the 19th century

Activity 9

In each of the following examples, the students are trying to move beyond descriptions of context so that their answers are more analytical. The first student has already been helped by the teacher. Read the teacher's advice for the other examples and then rewrite the student response.

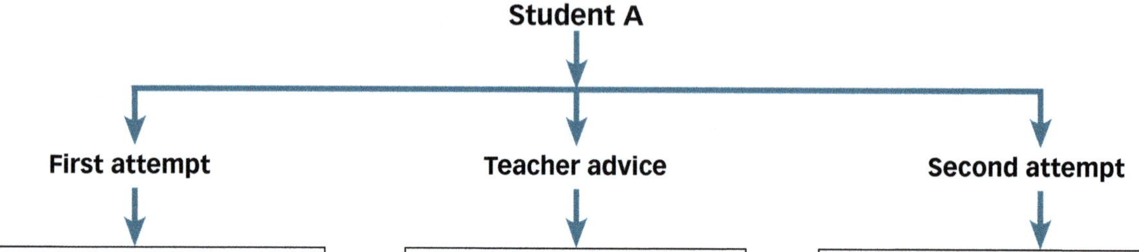

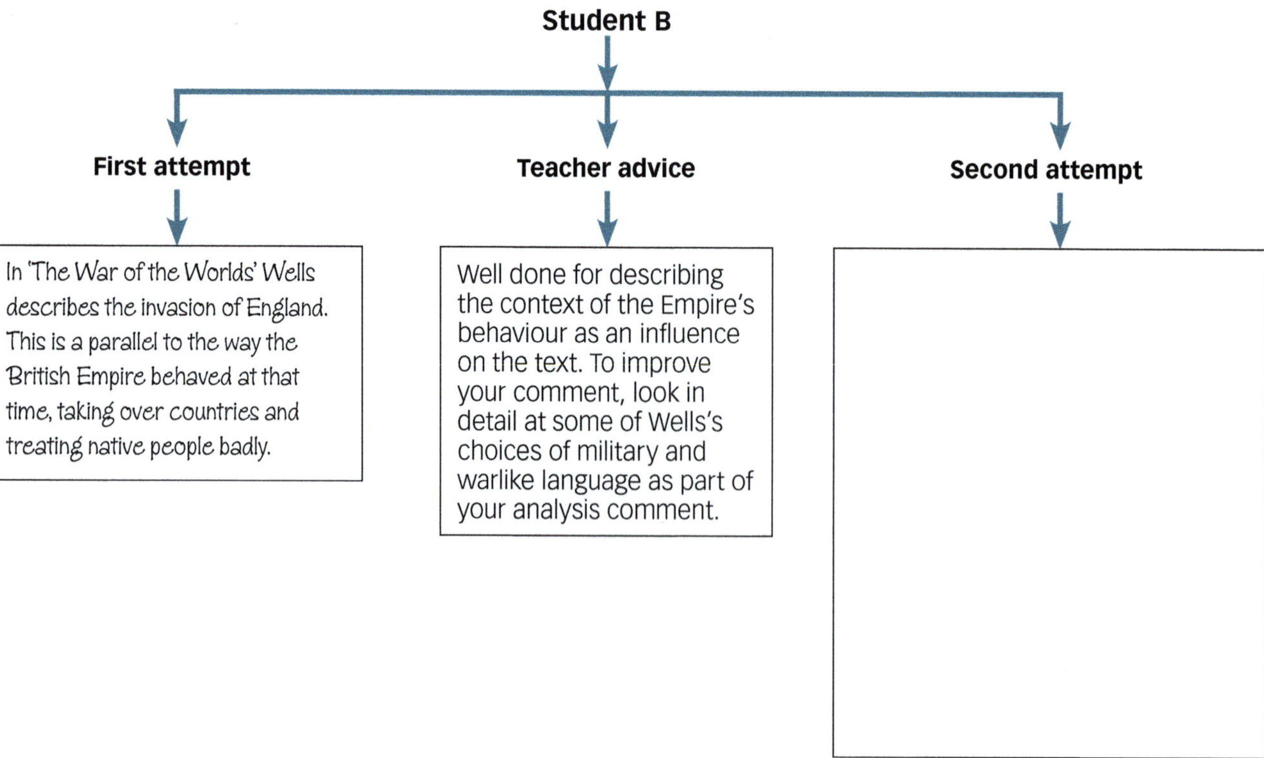

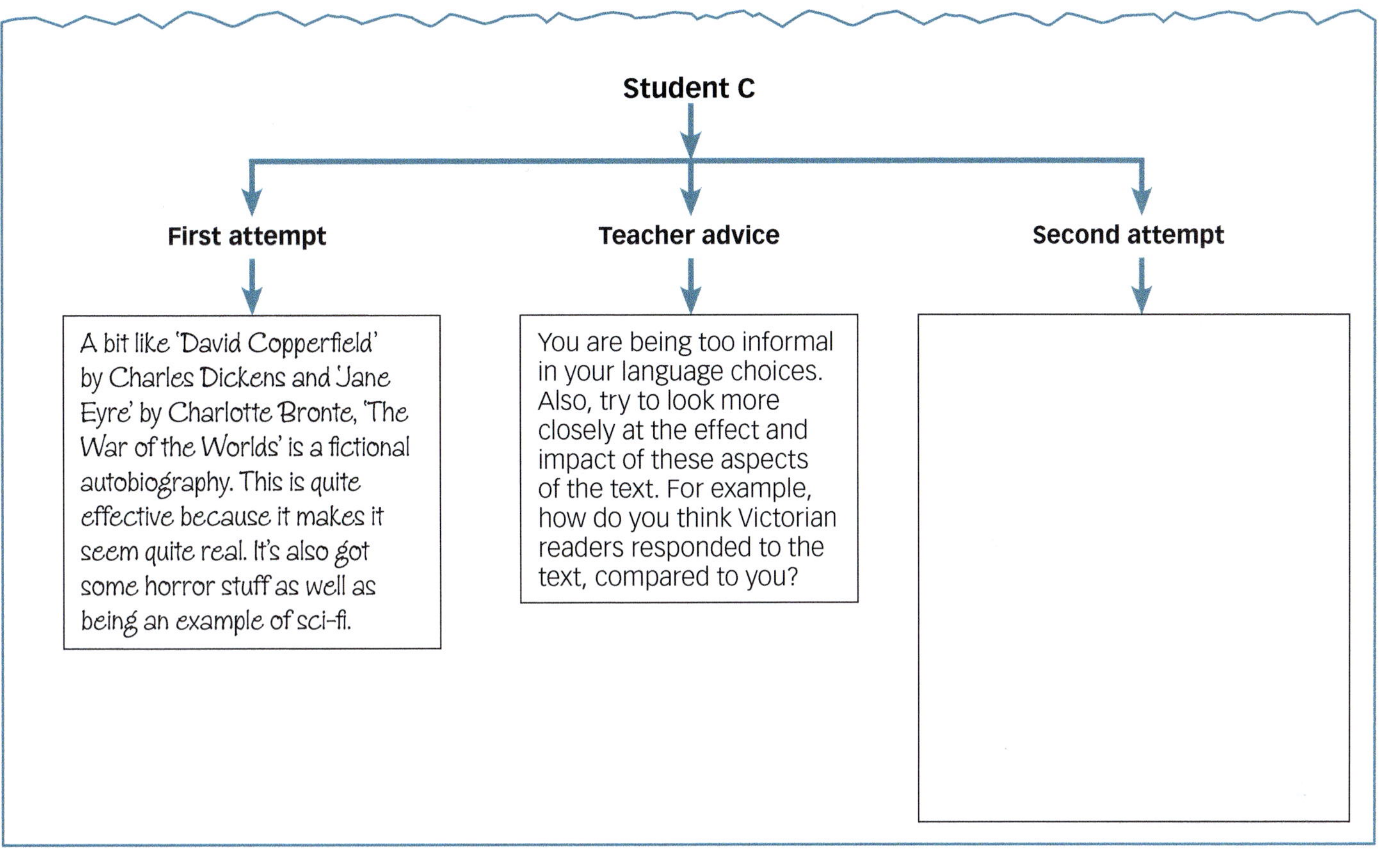

Progress check

Use the chart below to review the skills you have developed in this chapter. For each column, start at the bottom box and work your way up towards the highest level in the top box. Tick the box to show you have achieved that level.

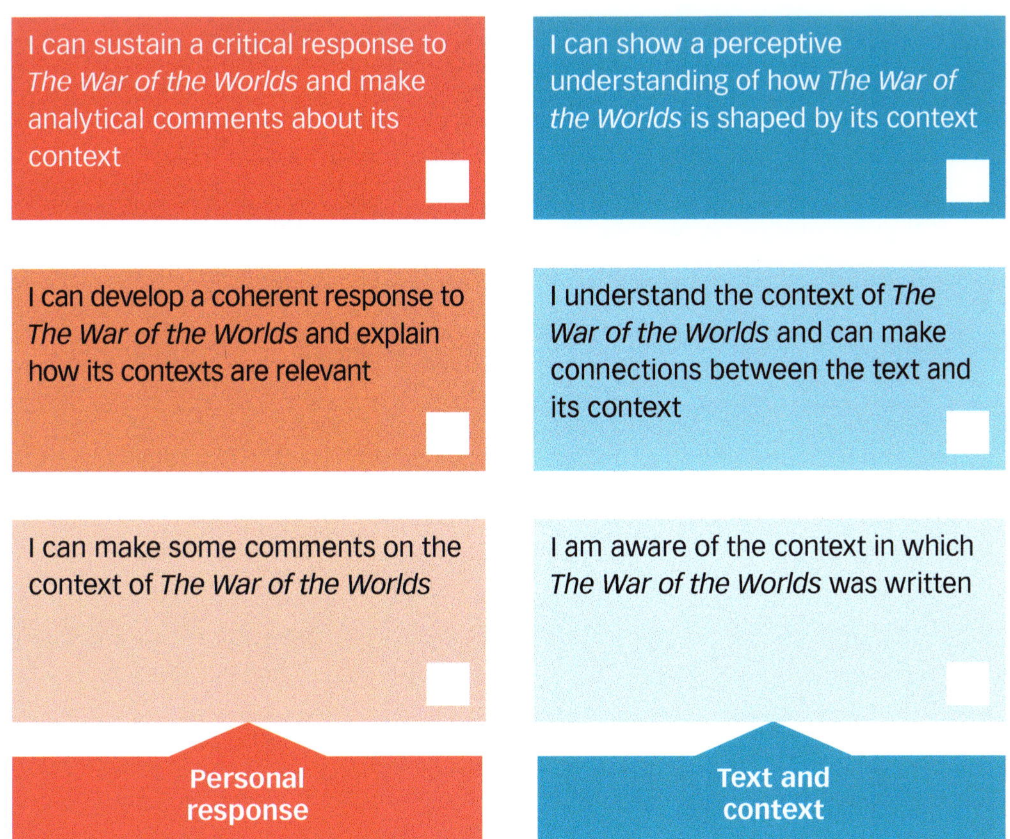

Character overview

Knowing the characters of any novel is an important part of knowing the whole text. In *The War of the Worlds,* there are very few characters whom we get to know in any depth, and a cast of minor characters who are used to help tell the story rather than because they are significant in themselves.

Activity 1

The chart below has been divided to show how the story is carried proportionally by different characters or groups of characters. The narrator, our chief **protagonist**, has one-third of the diagram (Section A) to himself. Decide which of the other characters, featured below, should go into the sections labelled 'main characters' or 'minor characters'.

> **protagonist** the main character in a work of fiction

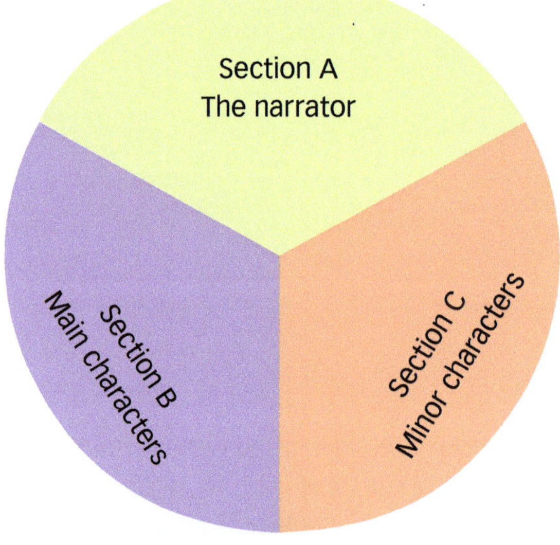

The narrator's wife

Ogilvy the astronomer

The artilleryman

The soldiers on Horsell Common

Miss Elphinstone

Ellen

The curate

The narrator's neighbour

A man with gold coins

The Leatherhead cousins

Lord Garrick

The landlord of the Spotted Dog pub

People in the boats at Weybridge

Mrs Elphinstone

Henderson the London journalist

The steamer captain

The narrator's brother

The narrator's milkman

Stent the Astronomer Royal

The Martians

Activity 2

On separate paper, make a set of character profile cards for the characters you have classified as main characters. On each card, include important information that will help with your revision, such as:

- first appearance
- key quotations
- relationship to narrator
- job, if stated
- purpose/importance to the plot
- final appearance.

Activity 3

To help you to think further about the characters, see how many ways you can think of to categorize them. Remember that one character may appear in more than one category. For example, 'Friendly to the narrator' is one category and 'Professional people' is another, and Ogilvy would fit in both these categories. Label the extra boxes according to your chosen categories and list the corresponding characters.

Friendly to the narrator	Professional people

The narrator

The most significant character in *The War of the Worlds* is the narrator himself. Our ability to understand the narrator is limited by the fact the story is told – even the parts that he does not directly witness – from his point of view. The next activities will help you to build your knowledge of him.

Activity 4

Search through your copy of the text to find out the following information about the narrator. You can write the answers in note form but try to use a combination of your own words and quotations from the text.

a) The narrator's job:

b) The narrator's most important relationships:

c) Two of the narrator's views of the Martians:

d) Two examples of the narrator's attitude to death:

e) How the narrator changes by the end of the novel:

Activity 5

To help see all the sides of the main character, the narrator, find some textual evidence to fit into each of the boxes on this mind map about him.

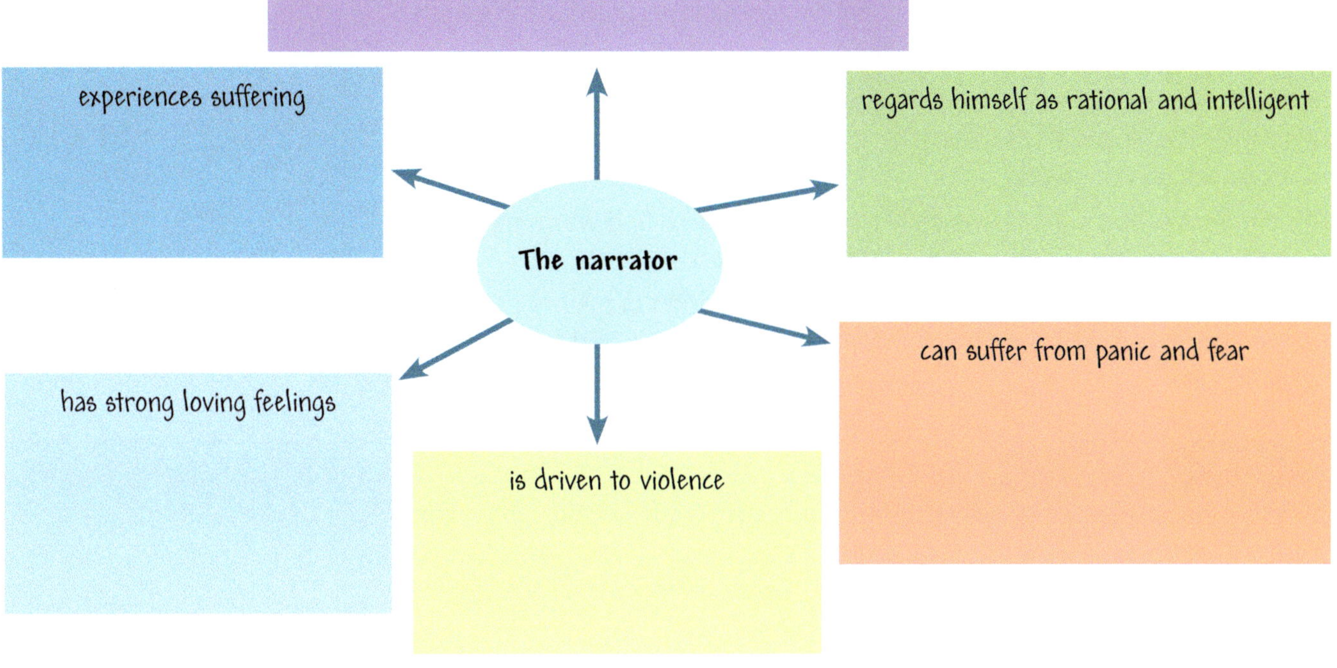

Activity 6

Choose one of the quotations below and explain how the narrator shows self-awareness and builds empathy for himself with the reader.

Quotation A

'A few minutes before, there had only been three real things before me – the immensity of the night and space and nature, my own feebleness and anguish, and the near approach of death. Now it was as if something turned over… I was immediately the self of every day again – a decent, ordinary citizen.' *(Book 1, Chapter 7)*

Quotation B

'… as the saying goes, I gripped myself with both hands. It grew upon my mind, once I could face the facts, that terrible as our position was, there was as yet no justification for absolute despair.' *(Book 2, Chapter 3)*

Nameless characters

Like so many of the characters in the story, the protagonist/main character remains unnamed. Here are a few different theories about why authors might choose to leave a character nameless.

1 Not naming a first-person narrator makes the reader associate the narrator character with the author.

2 Not giving a character a named identity means the author wants readers to view the character as an 'everyman' figure, representing humans in general.

3 Having a nameless main character creates more intrigue.

4 A character with no name may be perceived as having a crisis about their identity or dealing with massive change that has shifted their view of themselves and the world.

5 A nameless protagonist is less easy to empathize with and warm to, and sometimes authors want us to feel a little detached.

6 A nameless narrator can help suggest that observation of events and commenting on them is more important than storytelling and emotional connections.

Activity 7

Consider the six theories above about why authors might leave their characters nameless and decide what you think about this technique in *The War of the Worlds*. Write a short paragraph explaining your thoughts about why Wells chose to leave many of his characters, including the narrator, unnamed.

Activity 8

Like the narrator and his brother in this novel, the Martians are also nameless. Consider how different *The War of the Worlds* would be if H.G. Wells had chosen to alternate narrative voices, so that readers saw some events from the point of view of the invading enemy. Write a short invasion log entry in role as one of the Martians.

As the narrator is the protagonist and the Martians operate as the main **antagonist**, this is clearly an important relationship in the novel. However, there are other relationships that are significant, especially in the way Wells uses them to reveal information about the narrator and to draw attention to key ideas.

antagonist character opposing and challenging the protagonist

Activity 9

a) Consider the curate as an antagonist. Find two examples from the text in which the narrator and the curate are in conflict. In your own words, write a short description of their conflict. Try to make a link to religion, the main theme represented by the curate.

b) Consider the artilleryman as an antagonist. Find two examples from the text in which the narrator and the artilleryman are in conflict. In your own words, write a short description of their conflict. Try to make a link to eugenics, the main theme represented by the artilleryman.

What characters represent

Many of the characters in *The War of the Worlds* represent certain ideas or slices of society, rather than being fully rounded people with whom we empathize or with whom we can relate. A significant group of Wells's characters are experts in their field and function as **devices** in the novel rather than being fully developed. Wells also uses some characters as **symbols** to represent certain ideas.

> **device** a technique intended to produce a particular effect or fulfil a purpose in a literary work
>
> **symbol** when something or someone represents something else, such as an idea

 **Activity 10**

a) Draw lines between the columns to match up each character's name with their role and what they symbolize in the novel.

Character		Expert role		Symbol for
Ogilvy		Chief Justice		science, intelligence
Stent		London journalist		law, power, status
Henderson		Astronomer		the educated elite
Lord Garrick		Astronomer Royal		the wider world, the news media

b) Choose one of the characters listed above and use the notes from the chart to write a paragraph explaining the character, their role and what they symbolize. Include evidence in the form of a quotation.

For example, if you choose Ogilvy, you might start your paragraph like this:

Symbolizing the importance of science, Ogilvy plays a key part in the early chapters...

Activity 11

Use the following table to build your understanding of the characters, the ideas they represent and their purpose in the novel. A few spaces on the chart have been completed to help you.

Character	Social group or view represented	Purpose in novel	What Wells wants us to think about
The Elphinstone Ladies	Women: both older women like Mrs Elphinstone, who panics easily, and younger women like Miss Elphinstone, who is more modern and independent – for example, she shares watch duty with the narrator's brother		Women's point of view; how life for Victorian women changed at the end of the 19th century
The narrator's brother		To give the reader a wider view – for example, of how London is affected by the Martians' attack	
The curate			
Lord Garrick	Civilization, society, the law and powerful people in society		
The artilleryman			
Ogilvy			How even scientific advance and intelligence could fail to offer protection

Relationships

Knowing characters well and being able to describe and comment on their purpose is important. However, applying this knowledge of character, and writing with insight into how Wells uses characters to tell different aspects of the story or to reveal important ideas, is a key skill for the higher grades.

Upgrade

Wells shows the narrator as having important relationships with different characters in the novel. These relationships often change during the course of the story, revealing more about the narrator and sometimes changing his thinking and attitudes.

Activity 12

Complete these flow diagrams to pull together the key information about the narrator's main relationships. Some hints have been provided to help you with this task.

Martians

> **Narrator's first description**
>
> ------------------------------------
>
> ------------------------------------

↓

> **What the narrator learns over time**
>
> ------------------------------------
>
> ------------------------------------

↓

> **Nature of the relationship and how it changes or develops**
>
> ------------------------------------
>
> ------------------------------------

↓

> **What the relationship reveals about the narrator**
>
> ------------------------------------
>
> ------------------------------------

Hint 1: Use a combination of your own words and some short quotations from the relevant part of the text.

Hint 2: Try to use ideas from two or three other relevant parts of the text.

Hint 3: Try to sum up the relationship in a few key words. The following vocabulary choices might help: *aggressive, calming, challenging, safe, admiring, unstable, animosity, violent, influential, unsympathetic, disillusioned, happy, charged, condescending.*

Hint 4: Try out a range of phrases here to help you express the layers of meaning in your reading. For example:

This represents/symbolizes/suggests/implies…

The author intends/develops/illustrates/draws attention to…

The relationship exposes/highlights/emphasizes…

Curate

> **Narrator's first description** _
>
> _

> **What the narrator learns over time** _
>
> _

> **Nature of the relationship and how it changes or develops** _ _ _ _ _ _ _ _ _ _ _ _ _ _ _ _ _ _ _
>
> _

> **What the relationship reveals about the narrator** _
>
> _

Artilleryman

> **Narrator's first description** _
>
> _

> **What the narrator learns over time** _
>
> _

> **Nature of the relationship and how it changes or develops** _ _ _ _ _ _ _ _ _ _ _ _ _ _ _ _ _ _ _
>
> _

> **What the relationship reveals about the narrator** _
>
> _

Narrator's wife

> **Narrator's first description** ________________________________
>
> ________________________________

↓

> **What the narrator learns over time** ________________________________
>
> ________________________________

↓

> **Nature of the relationship and how it changes or develops** ________________________________
>
> ________________________________

↓

> **What the relationship reveals about the narrator** ________________________________
>
> ________________________________

Reading a text for understanding of characters and relationships requires 'reading between the lines'. This means identifying clues provided by the author and being aware of the implied or suggested meaning. These clues may come in the form of the language, the tone of voice or the events. For example, in the text extract that follows, the narrator describes an attack on an unknown man by the Martians, as observed by himself and the curate. Here we get clues about four different aspects of the narrator's character:

- his relationship with the curate
- his attitude to the Martians
- his feelings about humans in general, as represented by the captured man
- his view of himself.

I crouched, watching this fighting-machine closely, satisfying myself now for the first time that the hood did indeed contain a Martian. As the green flames lifted I could see the oily gleam of his integument[1] and the brightness of his eyes. And suddenly I heard a yell, and saw a long tentacle reaching over the shoulder of the machine to the little cage that hunched upon its back. Then something – something struggling violently – was lifted high against the sky, a black, vague enigma against the starlight; and as this black object came down again, I saw by the green brightness that it was a man. For an instant he was clearly visible. He was a stout, ruddy, middle-aged man, well dressed; three days before, he must have been walking the world, a man of considerable consequence. I could see his staring eyes and gleams of light on his studs and watch chain. He vanished behind the mound, and for a moment there was silence. And then began a shrieking and a sustained and cheerful hooting from the Martians.

I slid down the rubbish, struggled to my feet, clapped my hands over my ears, and bolted into the scullery. The curate, who had been crouching silently with his arms over his head, looked up as I passed, cried out quite loudly at my desertion of him, and came running after me.

That night, as we lurked in the scullery, balanced between our horror and the terrible fascination this peeping had, although I felt an urgent need of action I tried in vain to conceive some plan of escape; but afterwards, during the second day, I was able to consider our position with great clearness. The curate, I found, was quite incapable of discussion; this new and culminating atrocity had robbed him of all vestiges[2] of reason or forethought. Practically he had already sunk to the level of an animal. (*Book 2, Chapter 3*)

[1]integument – outer protective layer
[2]vestiges – traces, small amounts

Activity 13

Read the extract carefully and identify the words and phrases that provide the clues for each of the four aspects. The first one has been completed for you – note that you need to look throughout the extract and collect all the relevant words and phrases together.

Narrator's relationship with the curate	'crouching silently with his arms over his head' 'cried out quite loudly at my desertion of him, and came running after me' 'incapable of discussion' 'robbed him of all vestiges of reason' 'sunk to the level of an animal'
Narrator's attitude to the Martians	
Narrator's ideas about humans in general, as represented by the captured man	
Narrator's view of himself	

Critical understanding

Now that you have practised how to read between the lines when understanding character, you can use this information to write about how Wells presents his characters.

Activity 14

Read the extract again and then make notes on the character of the narrator using the colour-coded highlights and prompt questions to help you organize your ideas. Write your notes up into 2–3 paragraphs of textual analysis in the space provided on page 43.

Look at the words the narrator uses to describe his own actions.

1. a) How do his actions change during the passage?

   b) What do you think Wells wants us to think about the narrator at this point?

I crouched, watching this fighting-machine closely, satisfying myself now for the first time that the hood did indeed contain a Martian. As the green flames lifted I could see the oily gleam of his integument* and the brightness of his eyes. And suddenly I heard a yell, and saw a long tentacle reaching over the shoulder of the machine to the little cage that hunched upon its back. Then something – something struggling violently – was lifted high against the sky, a black, vague enigma against the starlight; and as this black object came down again, I saw by the green brightness that it was a man. For an instant he was clearly visible. He was a stout, ruddy, middle-aged man, well dressed; three days before, he must have been walking the world, a man of considerable consequence. I could see his staring eyes and gleams of light on his studs and watch chain. He vanished behind the mound, and for a moment there was silence. And then began a shrieking and a sustained and cheerful hooting from the Martians.

I slid down the rubbish, struggled to my feet, clapped my hands over my ears, and bolted into the scullery. The curate, who had been crouching silently with his arms over his head, looked up as I passed, cried out quite loudly at my desertion of him, and came running after me.

Look at the language the narrator uses for the man captured by the Martians.

2. a) What does this suggest about the narrator's ideas about people in general?

   b) How does he react to what happens to the man and why do you think Wells has written it this way?

Look at the way the Martians are described.

3. a) Decide whether the narrator is more admiring or revolted and explain your answer with reference to the text.

   b) What is Wells suggesting about the narrator's attitude to the Martians at this point?

That night, as we lurked in the scullery, balanced between our horror and the terrible fascination this peeping had, although I felt an urgent need of action I tried in vain to conceive some plan of escape; but afterwards, during the second day, I was able to consider our position with great clearness. The curate, I found, was quite incapable of discussion; this new and culminating atrocity had robbed him of all vestiges of reason or forethought. Practically he had already sunk to the level of an animal. (*Book 2, Chapter 3*)

Look at the way the narrator describes the curate.

4. a) On this evidence, what stage has their relationship reached?

   b) What does this suggest about Wells' views about the church's relevance in life?

In the next activity, you will apply skills of reading between the lines and interpreting character more independently through looking at a new piece of text. Read the steps below to remind yourself about how to read closely and effectively, and how to make notes in preparation for a response to a question.

Step 1: Read through the extract once for general meaning. If you know the book well, you will be able to make this a quick skim-read. Remind yourself where in the text the extract comes. Make a note of what has just happened and what is going to happen next.

Step 2: Reread with a focus. The focus will be determined by the question you are going to answer. Remember to read it and note any key words.

Step 3: Annotate the text with points that are relevant to the question and might help you put together an answer.

Step 4: Plan your answer. You could use a spider diagram or paragraph plan approach (see pages 86–87).

Step 5: Write your notes and annotations into coherent paragraphs using the formal tone and register of language that is appropriate for literary analysis.

Activity 15

a) Apply steps 1 and 2 to the extract and question below.

> Referring closely to the passage, explain the importance of the character of the narrator's brother.

At that time the road was crowded, but as yet far from congested. Most of the fugitives at that hour were mounted on cycles, but there were soon motor cars, hansom cabs, and carriages hurrying along, and the dust hung in heavy clouds along the road to St. Albans.

It was perhaps a vague idea of making his way to Chelmsford, where some friends of his lived, that at last induced my brother to strike into a quiet lane running eastward. Presently he came upon a stile, and, crossing it, followed a footpath north-eastward. He passed near several farmhouses and some little places whose names he did not learn. He saw few fugitives until, in a grass lane towards High Barnet, he happened upon two ladies who became his fellow travellers. He came upon them just in time to save them.

He heard their screams, and, hurrying round the corner, saw a couple of men struggling to drag them out of the little pony-chaise in which they had been driving, while a third with difficulty held the frightened pony's head. One of the ladies, a short woman dressed in white, was simply screaming; the other, a dark, slender figure, slashed at the man who gripped her arm with a whip she held in her disengaged hand.

My brother immediately grasped the situation, shouted, and hurried towards the struggle. One of the men desisted and turned towards him, and my brother, realizing from his antagonist's face that a fight was unavoidable, and being an expert boxer, went into him forthwith and sent him down against the wheel of the chaise. (*Book 1, Chapter 16*)

b) Use the following prompts to help you with step 3 (annotation of the text):

- What new information does the second-hand report of the narrator's brother bring to the narrator's limited account?
- Where and how does the narrator's brother behave differently to others?

Writing style

In your written responses to questions about *The War of the Worlds*, it is important to write in an appropriate formal, clear style. Here are some student responses that need improvement:

Student A

The character of the brother of the narrator is a bit of a devise and I reckon Wells included so that it wasn't quite so boring because only one of point of view is very samey and dull but with the narrator's brother you do get a chance to get to no other things like what it was like in London and all about the fight with the ship so it made it more exciting. But it would of been better if the narrator had mentioned his brother at the end.

Student B

The narrators brother is sort of important. though not much. He's only in a few chapters only. He helps the narrator tell us about stuff that happens in London and at the coast, where the narrator doesn't go himself.

Student C

The narrator is obsessed by class which isn't that surprising as this book was written in Victorian times when class was more of an issue. He calls poor people things like 'sturdy roughs'. The narrator's brother is quite like him but maybe a bit kinder. For example, he thinks quickly – he 'immediately grasped' the problem when the two Elphinstone women were being attacked and he fights for them, which shows he isn't less selfish than some of the people who only care about themselves, like the men who try to steal their pony and cart.

Activity 16

a) Identify the grammar, spelling and punctuation errors these writers have made by highlighting them. Note the corrections in the margins.

b) Using the table below, review the student answers against the success criteria for effective writing about character. Place ticks or crosses in the boxes accordingly.

Success criteria	Student A	Student B	Student C	My work
Correct spelling				
Appropriate formal and wide-ranging vocabulary, expression and correct grammar				
Comments on Wells's use of the character and his ideas				
Short quotations embedded				
Knowledge of the whole text shown by reference to a range of scenes				
Retelling the story avoided – events mentioned only briefly with much more focus on what they mean				

c) On separate paper, write your own paragraph of character analysis in response to one of the following:

i. How does Wells use the character of the curate?

ii. Why is the character of the artilleryman important?

When you have finished, use the chart on the previous page to check you have included all the desirable features.

Progress check

Use the chart below to review the skills you have developed in this chapter. For each column, start at the bottom box and work your way up towards the highest level in the top box. Tick the box to show you have achieved that level.

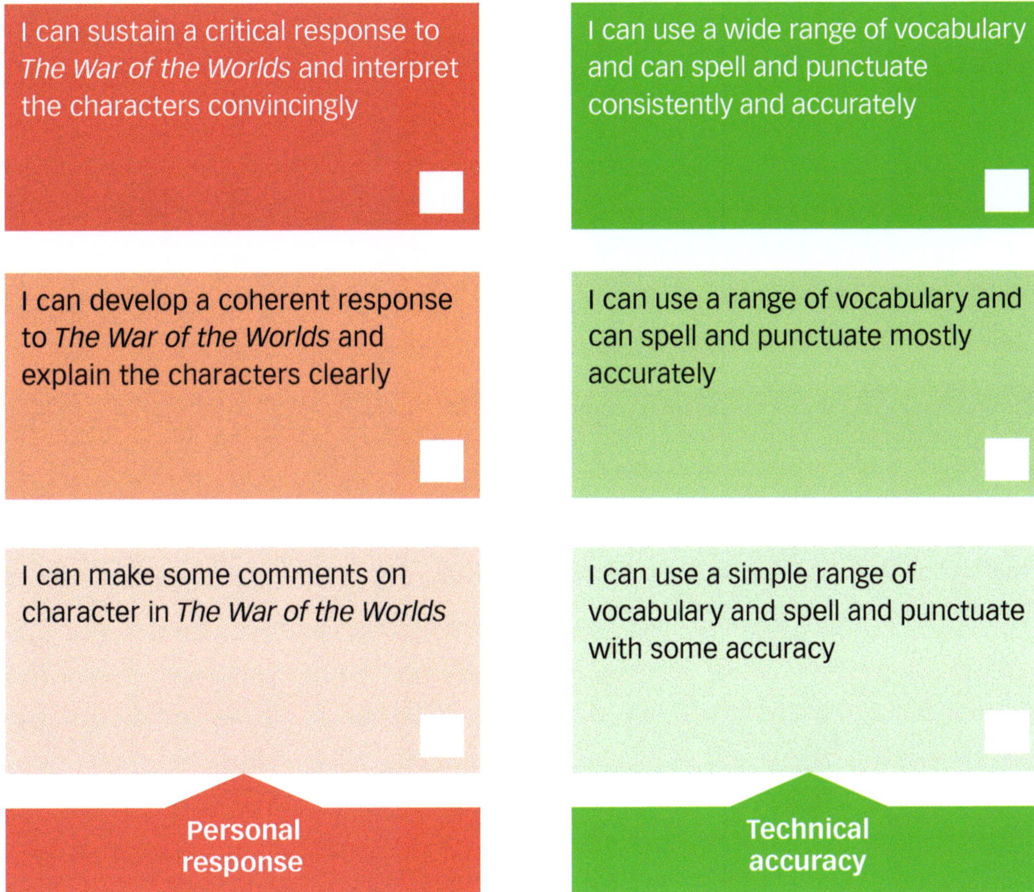

Layers of meaning

To write well about language, you need to develop the habit of reading closely, noticing details and looking beyond literal meanings to subtler, deeper layers of meaning. Literal meanings are obvious and clear, while deeper meanings often depend on links and associations that the reader may make or the way the author is suggesting or hinting at meaning, rather than telling the reader directly.

Activity 1

a) Read the following quotations and then match them to their literal meanings on page 49.

1

'All over the district people were dining and supping; working-men were gardening after the labours of the day, children were being put to bed, young people were wandering through the lanes love-making, students sat over their books.'
(Book 1, Chapter 8)

2

'Can you imagine a milking-stool tilted and bowled violently along the ground? That was the impression those instant flashes gave. But instead of a milking-stool imagine it a great body of machinery on a tripod stand.'
(Book 1, Chapter 10)

3

'…the curate cried faintly in his throat, and began running; but I knew it was no good running from a Martian, and I turned aside and crawled through dewy nettles and branches into the broad ditch by the side of the road.'
(Book 1, Chapter 15)

4

'Something rushed up into the sky out of the greyness – rushed slantingly upward and very swiftly into the luminous clearness above the clouds in the western sky; something flat and broad, and very large, that swept round in a vast curve, grew smaller, sank slowly, and vanished again into the grey mystery of the night. And as it flew it rained down darkness upon the land.'
(Book 1, Chapter 17)

Literal meaning

A description of an identified object flying through the air.

The narrator compares his own, cleverer reaction to the enemy with that of his companion.

The narrator is telling us that the Martians are not yet impacting on the lives of ordinary people.

The narrator is trying to describe the appearance of a moving Martian.

b) Now read the quotations again and match them to their subtle meanings.

Subtle meaning

Wells has the narrator talk directly to the ordinary reader using a comparison with a contemporary everyday object, which helps to make the extraordinary Martian invasion feel 'real' and credible.

Wells brings Book 1 to a close with a sense of mystery created through the repetition of 'something' and a biblical tone of doom.

Wells uses the narrator's commentary to hint at his intelligent and rational approach, compared to the more primitive instincts of others.

Wells reveals the narrator's sense of superiority over the masses – he is one of a tiny group who realize the significance of what is happening.

c) Now read the quotations below and identify both the literal and more subtle meanings. You will need to locate each quotation in the text to do this task well. Write your answers on separate paper.

1

'And in the evening many people came hurrying along the road nearby their stopping place, fleeing from unknown dangers before them, and going in the direction from which my brother had come.'
(Book 1, Chapter 16)

2

'Whenever I dozed I dreamt of horrible phantasms, of the death of the curate, or of sumptuous dinners; but, asleep or awake, I felt a keen pain that urged me to drink again and again.'
(Book 2, Chapter 5)

Narrative style

A fundamental aspect of *The War of the Worlds* is the narrative style. Its natural, realistic tone helps the reader to feel that the narrator is a real person. Sometimes, though, Wells purposefully undermines the naturalness of the novel with extremely literary and overblown language, reminding us that we are reading a novel – an artwork presenting an **apocalyptic** scenario that is only pretending to be a true account.

Wells achieves this through the following techniques:

- **First-person** limited point of view – the narrator's perspective dominates the novel, especially when he is explaining what he thinks. At times he does use the first-person plural ('we') to describe actions he carries out alongside others. The sections reported by the narrator's brother are written in the **third person**.

- **Journalistic** tone – a key factor in creating the naturalistic atmosphere of the novel is Wells's use of a personal, diary-style account. This means we focus on the narrator's chronological account of the events and facts.

- **Retrospective** account – Wells builds the relationship between the narrator and the reader by showing that the narrator can reflect on himself. Sometimes his reflections are rather smug and self-congratulatory; at other times they are self-critical and reveal honesty and awareness of his own weaknesses.

- Biblical language – this is used a lot by the curate but also by the narrator, thus creating links with the Bible that readers of the time would have been more familiar with than most modern readers. There are also **allusions** to specific Bible stories, and these give additional layers of meaning.

- Scientific and technical language – this helps to create an impression of authenticity, accuracy and reality. Wells includes high-level science jargon and technical descriptions throughout the novel.

allusion a reference made to something without naming it

apocalyptic referring to the end of the world

first person telling a story from the point of view of a narrating character, using the pronoun 'I'

journalistic in the style of a journal, with a detached, observational tone, focusing on facts and events

retrospective looking back on events and situations

third person using 'he', 'she', 'it', etc. to tell a story from another person's point of view

---

Key quotation

The planet Mars, I scarcely need remind the reader, revolves about the sun at a mean distance of 140,000,000 miles, and the light and heat it receives from the sun is barely half of that received by this world. It must be, if the nebular hypothesis has any truth, older than our world; and long before this earth ceased to be molten, life upon its surface must have begun its course.
(*Book 1, Chapter 1*)

Activity 2

Identify three short quotations, from across the novel as indicated, which illustrate the features of the narrator's style.

	Example from Book 1, Chapters 1–8	Example from Book 1, Chapters 9–17	Example from Book 2
First-person limited point of view			
Journalistic tone			
Retrospective account			
Biblical language			
Scientific and technical language			

Language features

To comment effectively on language, you need an understanding of the tools an author uses to create different effects. Here is an example extract from Book 2, Chapter 4, annotated to highlight the language features to look out for in any section of *The War of the Worlds*.

> **imagery** the use of visual or other vivid language to convey ideas and emotions

Fire symbolism – references to fire and its associations, e.g. superheated, scalded and scorched, symbolize the destruction carried out by the Martians.

Colour imagery – some colours are linked with particular ideas, e.g. red – a colour usually associated with danger – is linked to the Martians; black is linked to the idea of death.

Geographical reality – the text is packed with references to real places, which help to give it further real and journalistic qualities.

Natural and animalistic imagery – Wells makes comparisons or draws parallels between animals and humans, their behaviour and the impact the invasion has on them.

Time references – frequent references to the passing of time help to create the sense of an authentic and urgent experience, despite the fact that the narrator is reporting on the events of six years before.

Literary language – complementing and sometimes undermining the narrator's largely factual account, this language can be colourful, evocative and emotive.

Foreshadowing – giving the reader clues or warning about later events, creating intrigue and mystery.

Self-reflection – the narrator's references to his own learning and intelligence make him an apparently reliable observer, but sometimes make him seem rather pompous and snobbish.

A Martian came across the fields about midday, laying the stuff with a jet of superheated steam that hissed against the walls, smashed all the windows it touched, and scalded the curate's hand as he fled out of the front room. When at last we crept across the sodden rooms and looked out again, the country northward was as though a black snowstorm had passed over it. Looking towards the river, we were astonished to see an unaccountable redness mingling with the black of the scorched meadows.

For a time we did not see how this change affected our position, save that we were relieved of our fear of the Black Smoke. But later I perceived that we were no longer hemmed in, that now we might get away. So soon as I realized that the way of escape was open, my dream of action returned. But the curate was lethargic, unreasonable.

'We are safe here,' he repeated; 'safe here.'

I resolved to leave him – would that I had! Wiser now for the artilleryman's teaching, I sought out food and drink. I had found oil and rags for my burns, and I also took a hat and a flannel shirt that I found in one of the bedrooms. When it was clear to him that I meant to go alone – had reconciled myself to going alone – he suddenly roused himself to come. And all being quiet throughout the afternoon, we started about five o'clock, as I should judge, along the blackened road to Sunbury.

In Sunbury, and at intervals along the road, were dead bodies lying in contorted attitudes, horses as well as men, overturned carts and luggage, all covered thickly with black dust. That pall of cindery powder made me think of what I had read of the destruction of Pompeii. We got to Hampton Court without misadventure, our minds full of strange and unfamiliar appearances, and at Hampton Court our eyes were relieved to find a patch of green that had escaped the suffocating drift. We went through Bushey Park, with its deer going to and fro under the chestnuts, and some men and women hurrying in the distance towards Hampton, and so we came to Twickenham. These were the first people we saw. (*Book 2, Chapter 1*)

Activity 3

Use the annotations from the example on page 52 to help you analyse this new text extract. The arrows have been supplied to help you see where to focus.

That second start was the most foolhardy thing I ever did. For it was manifest the Martians were about us. No sooner had the curate overtaken me than we saw either the fighting-machine we had seen before or another, far away across the meadows in the direction of Kew Lodge. Four or five little black figures hurried before it across the green-grey of the field, and in a moment it was evident this Martian pursued them. In three strides he was among them, and they ran radiating from his feet in all directions. He used no Heat-Ray to destroy them, but picked them up one by one. Apparently he tossed them into the great metallic carrier which projected behind him, much as a workman's basket hangs over his shoulder.

It was the first time I realized that the Martians might have any other purpose than destruction with defeated humanity. We stood for a moment petrified, then turned and fled through a gate behind us into a walled garden, fell into, rather than found, a fortunate ditch, and lay there, scarce daring to whisper to each other until the stars were out.

I suppose it was nearly eleven o'clock before we gathered courage to start again, no longer venturing into the road, but sneaking along hedgerows and through plantations, and watching keenly through the darkness, he on the right and I on the left, for the Martians, who seemed to be all about us. In one place we blundered upon a scorched and blackened area, now cooling and ashen, and a number of scattered dead bodies of men, burned horribly about the heads and trunks but with their legs and boots mostly intact; and of dead horses, fifty feet, perhaps, behind a line of four ripped guns and smashed gun carriages.
(Book 2, Chapter 1)

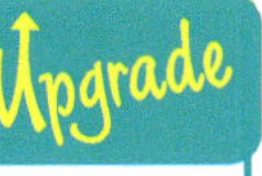

To access higher grades, you must give a full explanation of the effects of the language choices Wells has made. Just noting language features will not impress the examiner.

Developing your understanding of language

Interpreting layers of meaning as you did in Activity 1 is a good starting point for developing your understanding of language. However, for the higher grades you need to comment in detail on Wells's language choices, embedding quotations within your response.

Activity 4

To put your new awareness of some of Wells's language choices into practice, complete the table below.

a) Read the quotations in the first column carefully.

b) In the second column, write your own literal interpretation.

c) In the third column, devise your own comments on the deeper meanings or implications. To help with this, refer back to the notes on Wells's language choices over the past few pages. The first row has been completed as an example.

Quotations	Literal meaning	Deeper meaning and language choices
'He was a stout, ruddy, middle-aged man, well dressed; three days before, he must have been walking the world, a man of considerable consequence. I could see his staring eyes and gleams of light on his studs and watch chain. He vanished behind the mound, and for a moment there was silence. And then began a shrieking and a sustained and cheerful hooting from the Martians.' *(Book 2, Chapter 3)*	The narrator describes a man as he is trapped and killed by the Martians.	The background of the man who is killed is irrelevant to the Martians – he is just a food source to them. With the comment on the victim's status, Wells again reveals the narrator's deep-seated snobbery and awareness of the class system. The Martians' 'shrieking' and 'cheerful' reaction to their meal emphasizes the horrible disregard for life shown by the invaders.
'Strangest in this, that so soon as dawn had come, I, who had talked with God, crept out of the house like a rat leaving its hiding-place – a creature scarcely larger, an inferior animal, a thing that for any passing whim of our masters might be hunted and killed.' *(Book 2, Chapter 7)*		
'Before the cylinder fell there was a general persuasion that through all the deep of space no life existed beyond the petty surface of our minute sphere. Now we see further.' *(Book 2, Chapter 10)*		

Activity 5

Select your own quotation from the novel and write about your literal and deeper interpretation of it. Select your quotation with care – you need one that offers you the opportunity to show your literal understanding of the text, plus your ability to explain more subtle layers of meaning and to analyse Wells's use of language. Remember to embed some short quotations within your commentary.

The quotation I have chosen is

Learn by heart some short quotations that have interesting language features, which you may be able to use in your exam response.
Remember that short quotations can be as effective as longer ones.

Pathetic fallacy

The environment and the weather feature heavily in the narrator's descriptions. Wells uses a technique called **pathetic fallacy**, exploiting the natural environment to enhance the atmosphere created in the story.

pathetic fallacy a literary technique that gives human qualities or emotions to natural events, such as the weather, to reflect a particular mood

> **Key quotation**
>
> It was glaringly hot, not a cloud in the sky nor a breath of wind, and the only shadow was that of the few scattered pine trees. The burning heather had been extinguished, but the level ground towards Ottershaw was blackened as far as one could see, and still giving off vertical streamers of smoke.
> *(Book 1, Chapter 3)*

Activity 6

a) Match the events, listed 1-4 below, with the natural conditions described in the table.

  1 The narrator emerges from his imprisonment in the ruined house.

  2 The narrator looks at the dead Martians.

  3 The narrator and his wife go for a walk before the Martians arrive.

  4 The narrator returns to Maybury after taking his wife to the Leatherhead cousins.

Natural conditions	Event	Why is the choice of natural conditions significant at this moment?
Starlight on a warm night *(Book 1, Chapter 1)*		
A thunderstorm *(Book 1, Chapter 10)*		
A sunny day with a gentle breeze *(Book 2, Chapter 5)*		
A summer sunrise *(Book 2, Chapter 8)*		

b) In the third column, explain why Wells's choice of weather and time is significant at that moment.

Biblical language

Wells uses a range of biblical language in the novel, much of which would have been immediately recognized by readers at the time the book was published. The biblical references are echoes of Wells's own religious upbringing and they often help to create an apocalyptic tone.

Activity 7

Find three examples of biblical language from across the text, and write a short comment about each. You might like to consider:

- how the biblical references create a prophetic or warning tone
- what associations the biblical language puts in readers' minds
- whether the biblical references suggest that Wells is positive about faith, or not.

a) Biblical language example 1

b) Biblical language example 2

c) Biblical language example 3

Analysing language

Another significant language feature in *The War of the Worlds* is Wells's references to food. He uses these references for a variety of reasons, for example:

- to help depict normal life and routines
- when food is scarce, indicating another layer of jeopardy for the characters
- as commentary on the eating habits of the Martians.

Read the student answer below. It is in response to the question: 'How does Wells use food in *The War of the Worlds*?'

Wells makes frequent references to food in the novel. Sometimes it is to tell us about normal daily life, such as the breakfast that Ogilvy and Henderson have near the beginning. This helps to increase the sense of the negative impact that the Martians have on Earth when all these normal meal experiences have to change. Also, Wells often uses food to help create tension, like when the narrator's neighbour gives him 'a handful of strawberries' just before the Martians start setting fire to everyone. Strawberries symbolize the beauty and sweetness of summer, and so it is ironic that the narrator receives some on such an apocalyptic day.

Another use of food is to demonstrate the narrator's despair and how bad things become. At two different, very challenging moments in Book 2, he describes eating 'some fronds of red weed' and 'crushed and scattered' animal bones. This shows how low the narrator has sunk from the picture he presents of himself at the beginning of the novel, when he came across as an educated and learned person. In these examples, the word used for eating is 'gnawed', which goes even further, implying that the narrator has become like an animal in his hunger and desperation.

This response is strong because it:

1 makes a range of points, e.g. food as routine/food as a symbol/food to show characterization
2 gives examples from the text and uses embedded quotations
3 links ideas together with cohesive devices, e.g. 'another use of'/'also'/'which goes even further'
4 refers to different parts of the novel, e.g. 'beginning', 'Book 2'
5 is written accurately and formally, expressing ideas clearly, e.g. 'frequent references'/'symbolize the beauty and sweetness of summer'
6 comments on the significance of Wells's language choices, e.g. 'to create tension'/'shows how low the narrator has sunk'/'implying that the narrator has become like an animal'.

Activity 8

Annotate the student's work to identify where each strength (1 to 6, opposite) can be seen. Draw lines to point to where that skill is demonstrated in the essay extract.

Many students find that the most challenging skill listed on page 58 is commenting on the significance of Wells's language choices. Doing this well may include:

- suggesting extra layers of meaning of a particular word
- making a link between language and impact on the reader
- explaining the symbolic significance of the language chosen
- linking language to context or theme
- highlighting how language contributes to character or atmosphere.

Upgrade

Strong exam answers show good literary analysis skills and display these skills in a well-argued and coherent way. Try to use cohesive devices to link together your sentences and paragraphs in a logical, flowing manner. See below for some examples of useful cohesive devices.

At the beginning of a paragraph:

Another point…

A different view is…

Wells also…

To deepen analysis within a paragraph:

Looking at this more deeply…

Another way of looking at this is…

This also has the effect of…

Activity 9

Write at least one more paragraph for the student answer on page 58 about how
Wells uses references to food in *The War of the Worlds*. Here are the student's notes
to help you.

Activity 10

Assess the strengths and weaknesses of your paragraph, referring to the bullet list below. Annotate your writing to highlight possible improvements, then write a final draft on a separate sheet of paper.

- Giving examples from the text and using embedded quotations ☐
- Linking ideas together with cohesive devices ☐
- Referring to different parts of the novel ☐
- Writing accurately and formally, expressing ideas clearly ☐

Progress check

Use the chart below to review the skills you have developed in this chapter. For each column, start at the bottom box and work your way up towards the highest level in the top box. Tick the box to show you have achieved that level.

I can sustain a critical response to *The War of the Worlds* and interpret the language convincingly ☐	I can analyse the effects of Wells' use of language, structure and form in *The War of the Worlds*, using subject terms judiciously ☐
I can develop a coherent response to *The War of the Worlds* and explain Wells' use of language clearly ☐	I can explain how Wells uses language, structure and form to create effects in *The War of the Worlds*, using relevant subject terms ☐
I can make some comments on the language features of *The War of the Worlds* ☐	I can identify some of Wells' methods in *The War of the Worlds* and use some subject terms ☐
Personal response	**Language, structure, form**

Themes

Key ideas

Wells considers several **themes** in the novel and it's important to have a good understanding of them.

theme a subject or idea that is repeated or developed in a literary work

Activity 1

Complete the following spider diagram showing some of the themes of the novel.

a) Identify a relevant moment from the text for each one.

b) Write a short note about the moment you have chosen, using the completed example as a guide.

Activity 2

a) Consider the themes below. Decide which you think are the most important in *The War of the Worlds* and place them on the ladder, with the most important at the top and the least important at the bottom.

Fate versus free will   Fear   Humanity and community   Imperialism

Science and technology   Morality   Nature   Religion

The future   War

b) Write a short paragraph explaining why you think your number 1 theme is the most important in the novel. Include some close references to the text.

1

2

3

4

5

6

7

8

9

10

Creating a bank of quotations to help you explore the main themes in the text will be a useful revision task. In the next activity, you will need to skim-read the novel again. Rereading the text will help you get to know it thoroughly and enable you to write about it with confidence.

Activity 3

a) Choose a quotation from page 65 that links to each theme listed in the table below. Write it, or a key part of it, in the second column.

b) Then skim-read the novel to find another quotation to link to each theme and write it in the third column.

c) Highlight key words and phrases in the quotations that you could memorize and use in an exam response.

Theme	Quotation 1 (from page 65)	Quotation 2 (from your own research)
War		
Fate versus free will		
Fear		
Humanity and community		
Imperialism		
Morality		
Nature		
Religion		
Science and technology		
The future		

"You are scared out of your wits! What good is religion if it collapses under calamity? Think of what earthquakes and floods, wars and volcanoes, have done before to men! Did you think God had exempted Weybridge? He is not an insurance agent."
(Book 1, Chapter 13)

'And before we judge of them too harshly we must remember what ruthless and utter destruction our own species has wrought, not only upon animals, such as the vanished bison and the dodo, but upon its inferior races.' *(Book 1, Chapter 1)*

'I felt the first inkling of a thing that presently grew quite clear in my mind, that oppressed me for many days, a sense of dethronement, a persuasion that I was no longer a master, but an animal among the animals, under the Martian heel.' *(Book 2, Chapter 6)*

'I saw myself then as I see myself now, driven step by step towards that hasty blow, the creature of a sequence of accidents leading inevitably to that. I felt no condemnation; yet the memory, static, unprogressive, haunted me.' *(Book 2, Chapter 7)*

'Several officers from the Inkerman barracks had been on the common earlier in the day, and one, Major Eden, was reported to be missing. The colonel of the regiment came to the Chobham bridge and was busy questioning the crowd at midnight.' *(Book 1, Chapter 8)*

'The Martians had what appears to have been an auditory organ, a single round drum at the back of the head-body, and eyes with a visual range not very different from ours…' *(Book 2, Chapter 2)*

'Those who have escaped the dark and terrible aspects of life will find my brutality, my flash of rage in our final tragedy, easy enough to blame; for they know what is wrong as well as any, but not what is possible to tortured men.' *(Book 2, Chapter 3)*

'Troubled as they were with their own affairs, these people, whose name, much as I would like to express my gratitude to them, I may not even give here, nevertheless cumbered themselves with me, sheltered me, and protected me from myself.' *(Book 2, Chapter 9)*

'We have learned now that we cannot regard this planet as being fenced in and a secure abiding place for Man; we can never anticipate the unseen good or evil that may come upon us suddenly out of space.' *(Book 2, Chapter 10)*

'After the glimpse I had had of the Martians emerging from the cylinder in which they had come to the earth from their planet, a kind of fascination paralyzed my actions. I remained standing knee-deep in the heather, staring at the mound that hid them. I was a battleground of fear and curiosity.' *(Book 1, Chapter 5)*

Linking themes

You have probably noticed that many of the themes in *The War of the Worlds* are interlinked. For example, you can start off looking at the idea of fear, which might lead you to the theme of the future and then to the notion of science. We could show this in a flow chart:

> **Fear** is a key theme in the novel. Wells shows it in many ways, from the frightened people at the edge of the pit at the beginning, to the final chapter when the narrator is worrying about the future.

> **Future** In the final chapter, the narrator describes his bad dreams and his anxiety about 'the possibility of another attack'. Wells is demonstrating the Victorian interest in new ideas; he was writing at the end of the 19th century when it would have been natural to think about change and scientific development.

> **Science** Wells was a scientist and he was particularly interested in new research into space and technology and how these might impact on humanity in the future. The novel makes some fascinatingly accurate predictions about modern life, including space travel and weapons of mass destruction.

Activity 4

Use the templates provided to create your own flow charts to show how ideas link together. You can insert your own choice of theme trios, or use these suggested ideas:

Relationships ⟶ community and humanity ⟶ morality

War ⟶ imperialism ⟶ religion

Recognizing and tracking themes

Remember that themes are ideas that crop up again and again in a text. They are usually introduced in the early pages, and then referred to and developed as the novel goes on. But they may not always be obvious – Wells may represent the ideas in different ways, through symbols, characters and events or actions.

Activity 5

Match up the events or actions listed on the left with the idea each stands for on the right, as in the example shown.

Event or action	Theme
The narrator kills the curate (*Book 2, Chapter 4*).	Imperialism and war
The narrator compares himself to a rabbit (*Book 2, Chapter 6*).	Science
A company of soldiers advances to Horsell Common (*Book 1, Chapter 8*).	Religion
The narrator thinks about what will happen in years to come (*Book 2, Chapter 10*).	Nature
The Martians are reported to be learning to fly (*Book 2, Chapter 7*).	The future

Tracking themes as they develop chapter by chapter should be an important element of your revision of the text, because it will reinforce your understanding that the ideas are not static or simplistic. For example, you want to progress from a simple statement like 'Wells explores the idea of democracy in the novel' to making a more thoughtful comment, such as 'Wells presents democracy as a fragile concept and shows how easily it is destroyed.'

Activity 6

Choose three themes and find references to them in at least four different chapters. Make brief notes about each reference in the table below, focusing on how that idea or theme is developed. One example has been completed as a guide. Try to embed a relevant quotation in your commentary.

Themes	References
Imperialism	1. Book 1, Chapter 1: **'With infinite complacency men went to and fro over this globe about their little affairs, serene in their assurance of their empire over matter.'** The book opens with a reminder of the imperial attitude of the Victorian age, when some places in the world were systematically colonized and controlled by others.
	2. Book 1, Chapter 10: **'Something very like the war-fever that occasionally runs through a civilized community had got into my blood.'** Later, Wells develops the idea of imperialism, showing that even the narrator is not immune to it. He contrasts the idea of civilization with 'war-fever', perhaps suggesting that decent societies do not wish to dominate others.
	3. Book 2, Chapter 6: **'… I was no longer a master, but an animal among the animals, under the Martian heel. With us it would be as with them, to lurk and watch, to run and hide; the fear and empire of man had passed away.'** As the Martian invasion continues, the narrator reflects on his new role as an underdog, a member of a society that has lost its power and control.
	4. Book 2, Chapter 8: **'I thought of the multitudinous hopes and efforts, the innumerable hosts of lives that had gone to build this human reef, and of the swift and ruthless destruction that had hung over it all.'** Towards the end of the novel, the narrator realizes that the Martian attack is over but considers how fragile humanity is. Wells seems to be questioning the destruction that Britons had been part of in his lifetime.

Themes	References
	1.
	2.
	3.
	4.
	1.
	2.
	3.
	4.
	1.
	2.
	3.
	4.

Writing about themes

Once you know how to track the development of ideas, you will be able to write effectively and analytically about Wells's themes. For example, here is the beginning of a sample student answer to the question: 'How does Wells present ideas about fate and free will?'

You can see the strong points of this response from the teacher's comments.

Effective use of key words related to the question

Comment on Wells' language – well done

Excellent comments on the author's intentions

Relevant quotations embedded

Good – a brief reference to the plot without retelling the story

> Wells explores ideas of fate and free will from early in the novel. In the first chapter, the narrator reflects on the lack of control men have over their own destiny: he describes how men were 'serene in their assurance of their empire over matter', but their sense of superiority was wiped away by the Martians' planned attack when 'the storm burst upon us'. This idea of man's control of life being completely threatened by external events recurs throughout the book. At the end of Chapter 2, for example, the narrator imagines Ogilvy and Henderson 'covered with sand, excited and disordered, running up the little street'. Using words that emphasise lack of control, Wells seems to be saying that even professional, intelligent, educated men are not in charge of their own fate. This idea crops up again later when the narrator describes how he stands 'motionless, dumbfounded and dazzled' as the first Heat-Ray is released. He himself is 'passed and spared' – but only by luck, because many others are killed.

Activity 7

Use one of the following question templates to write your own question around a theme – you need to insert the theme you want to write about in the space.

- What are Wells' ideas about _________________ and how does he show its different sides?
- How does Wells present the narrator's experience of _________________?
- Referring to three different parts of the novel, explain Wells' attitudes to _________________ .

Activity 8

Write the opening paragraph of an answer to the question you created in Activity 7. Try to incorporate the strengths of the writing in the student answer above. Continue on separate paper if you need to.

Of course, at any single moment in the novel, multiple themes might be referenced. This means you need to read carefully, and notice how Wells intertwines references to a range of ideas.

Activity 9

Read the following extract and note the different themes that Wells touches on. Identify where each theme is relevant in the extract by inserting arrows to key words and phrases. Then, for each theme, add a short explanation in the text boxes to explain how it is relevant at this point in the novel. Use the example given as a model.

Fate and free will
The people do not seem to have any control over their movements.

Community and humanity

Religion

One man's hands pressed on the back of another. My brother stood at the pony's head. Irresistibly attracted, he advanced slowly, pace by pace, down the lane.

Edgware had been a scene of confusion, Chalk Farm a riotous tumult, but this was a whole population in movement. It is hard to imagine that host. It had no character of its own. The figures poured out past the corner, and receded with their backs to the group in the lane. Along the margin came those who were on foot, threatened by the wheels, stumbling in the ditches, blundering into one another.

The carts and carriages crowded close upon one another, making little way for those swifter and more impatient vehicles that darted forward every now and then when an opportunity showed itself of doing so, sending the people scattering against the fences and gates of the villas.

'Push on!' was the cry. 'Push on! They are coming!'

In one cart stood a blind man in the uniform of the Salvation Army, gesticulating with his crooked fingers and bawling, 'Eternity! Eternity!' His voice was hoarse and very loud so that my brother could hear him long after he was lost to sight in the dust. Some of the people who crowded in the carts whipped stupidly at their horses and quarrelled with other drivers; some sat motionless, staring at nothing with miserable eyes; some gnawed their hands with thirst, or lay prostrate in the bottoms of their conveyances. The horses' bits were covered with foam, their eyes bloodshot. (*Book 1, Chapter 16*)

Fear

Nature

Activity 10

a) Use your annotations in Activity 9 as a starting point to write a response to the question 'In the extract, how does Wells explore key ideas?'

----

b) Review your work and check that you have:

- used cohesive devices to make your argument flow (see page 59)

- referred closely to the text

- integrated short quotations.

Activity 11

Now apply the same type of annotations as you developed in Activity 9 (naming themes and explaining their relevance) to the extract from the novel below. This time, you need to identify the multiple thematic references that Wells is making on your own.

As the dawn grew clearer, we saw through the gap in the wall the body of a Martian, standing sentinel, I suppose, over the still glowing cylinder. At the sight of that we crawled as circumspectly as possible out of the twilight of the kitchen into the darkness of the scullery.

Abruptly the right interpretation dawned upon my mind.

'The fifth cylinder,' I whispered, 'the fifth shot from Mars, has struck this house and buried us under the ruins!'

For a time the curate was silent, and then he whispered:

'God have mercy upon us!'

I heard him presently whimpering to himself.

Save for that sound we lay quite still in the scullery; I for my part scarce dared breathe, and sat with my eyes fixed on the faint light of the kitchen door. I could just see the curate's face, a dim, oval shape, and his collar and cuffs. Outside there began a metallic hammering, then a violent hooting, and then again, after a quiet interval, a hissing like the hissing of an engine. These noises, for the most part problematical, continued intermittently, and seemed if anything to increase in number as time wore on. Presently a measured thudding and a vibration that made everything about us quiver and the vessels in the pantry ring and shift, began and continued. Once the light was eclipsed, and the ghostly kitchen doorway became absolutely dark. For many hours we must have crouched there, silent and shivering, until our tired attention failed… (*Book 2, Chapter 1*)

Activity 12

a) Write up your annotations on the text on page 73 into a paragraph to answer the question 'In the extract, how does Wells explore key ideas?'

----

b) Review your paragraph and check that you have answered the 'how' part of the question. This means you will have commented on the way that Wells writes. For example, you might have mentioned how the ideas or themes are developed by:

- vocabulary choice
- creation of mood or atmosphere
- character development
- sentence structure.

Upgrade

Practise this skill of identifying themes in different extracts. Just choose other passages and apply the same technique. If you have your own copy of the novel, you may find it helpful to use highlighters to colour-code different themes. A thorough knowledge of the novel's themes will be an asset in most exam responses.

Progress check

Use the chart below to review the skills you have developed in this chapter. For each column, start at the bottom box and work your way up towards the highest level in the top box. Tick the box to show you have achieved that level.

I can sustain a critical response to *The War of the Worlds* and interpret the themes convincingly ☐

I can develop a coherent response to *The War of the Worlds* and explain the themes clearly ☐

I can make some comments on the themes in *The War of the Worlds* ☐

Personal response

I can use well-integrated textual references from *The War of the Worlds* to support my interpretation ☐

I can use quotations and other textual references from *The War of the Worlds* to support my explanation ☐

I can make references to some details from *The War of the Worlds* ☐

Textual references

Understanding questions

Doing your best in any exam is all about preparation. After your close reading of *The War of The Worlds* and working through this book, you should be feeling confident about the sorts of things you will write about. In this section, you will prepare for different sorts of exam questions, practise writing answers and review sample responses that you can learn from.

Activity 1

Complete the table below by formulating another example question using each key question word or phrase. You will find that some exam question words crop up again and again.

Key exam question word or phrase	What do you have to do?	Example question	Your own example question
Explore…	Investigate openly and write about a range of different ideas.	Explore the role of the narrator's brother in the novel as a whole.	
Explain…	Put forward different views, with reasons to justify them.	Explain the importance of the colour red in the novel.	
In what ways…	Present a range of ideas and explain them.	In what ways is the character of the curate significant?	
How far… /To what extent…	Evaluate the level or amount of something.	To what extent does Wells criticize humanity in the novel?	
How does Wells…	Examine the techniques the author uses.	How does Wells create drama in this extract?	

Making up your own questions and writing essay plans and whole answers is a great revision activity. Try to do this more as you get closer to the exam, setting yourself the same time limit you will have in the exam.

In the exam, avoid launching straight into writing your answer. Make sure you really understand what the question is asking. Pay attention to the key question words and remind yourself what they mean. Turning the exam question into a mini spider diagram is a good way to help you focus on what is being asked and to start planning. Here is an example.

Investigate and write about a range of ideas – think about what different characters say about science. Need to include positives and negatives

Focus on the language and techniques the author uses – voices of different characters, positive and negative imagery about science, linking science to learning and education

Explore how Wells presents attitudes to science and technology.

Include different points of view about this theme – the narrator's fascination with science; the Martians representing technological advances; the artilleryman's comments.

Activity 2

Using the example above as a guide, explore each of these possible exam questions with mini spider diagrams.

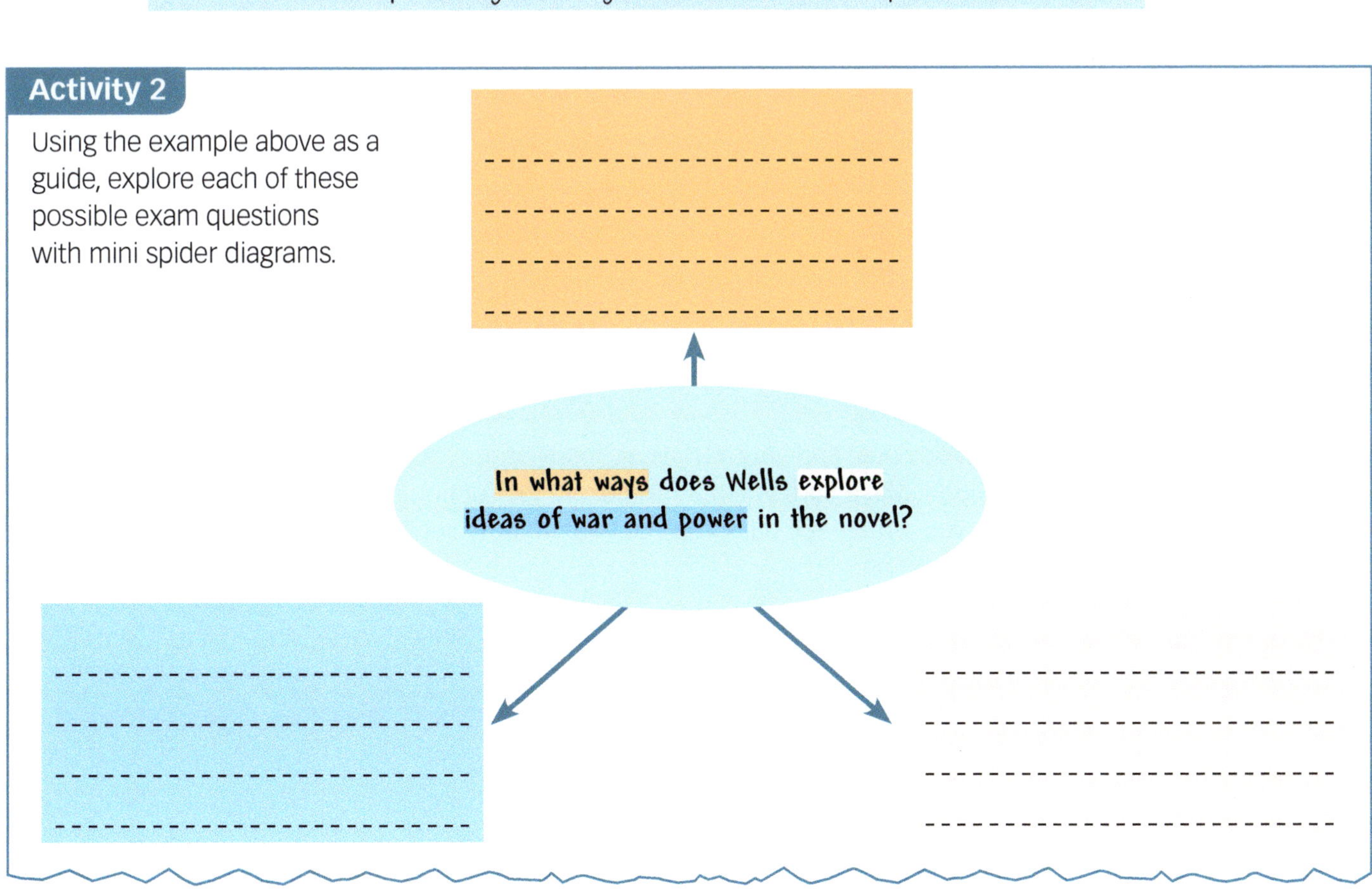

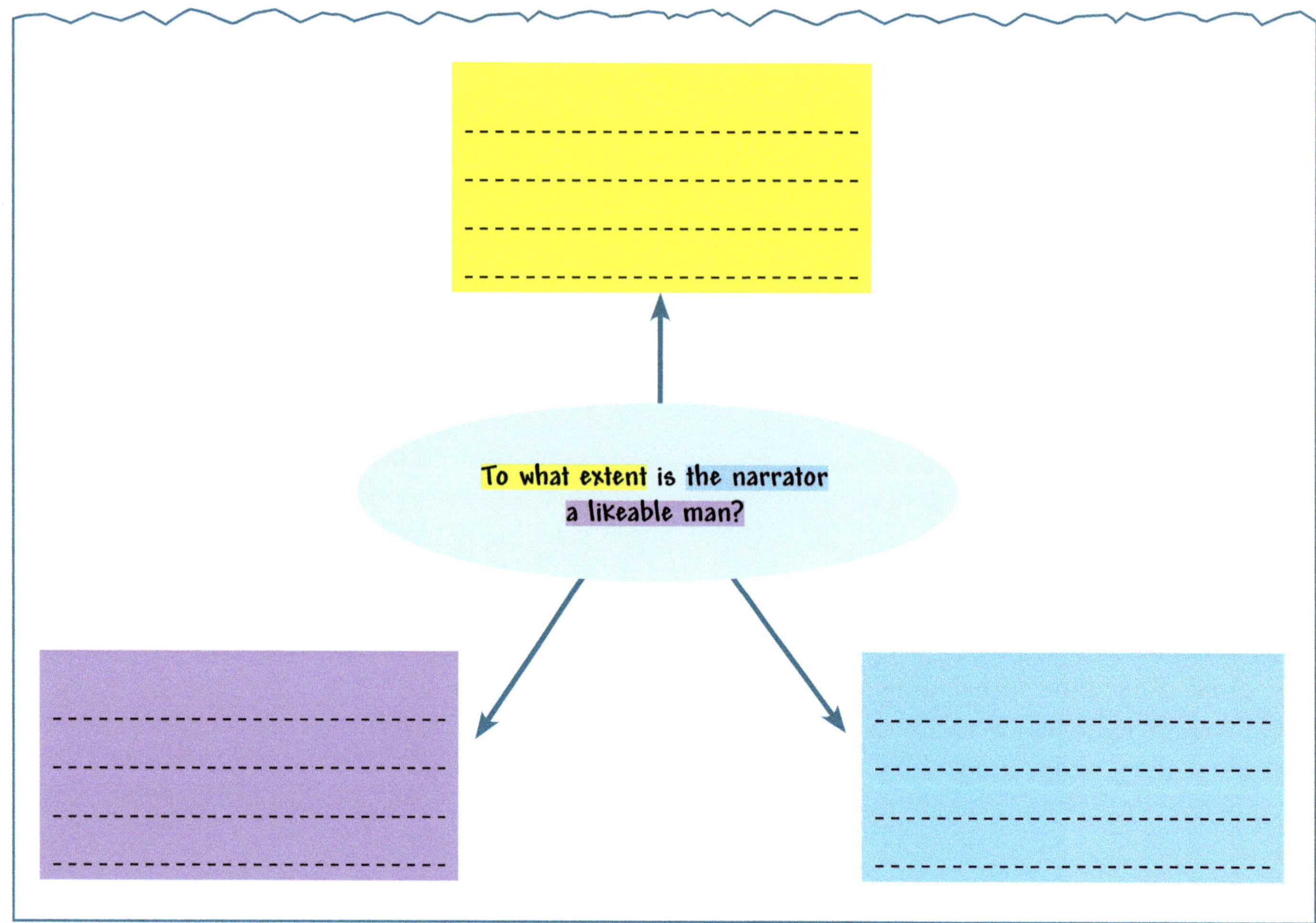

Exam techniques

Sometimes things go wrong in exams. This isn't surprising, because people are under pressure and it's easy to make mistakes. But being well-prepared includes having good exam techniques. For example, you must:

- read the question at least three times
- use some of the time allowed to plan your answer – and don't cross it out, as you may be given credit for things you've included in your plan
- make sure your grammar, punctuation and spelling are the best they can be – there are some marks for this
- answer the question!

This last piece of advice sounds so obvious, and yet every year, many students go wrong by not answering the question. Make sure you read the exam instructions and the question carefully and as you write each paragraph of your answer keep checking that it is focused on the question.

Getting started

Four students are in a panic as their exams start and they are each about to make a classic mistake.

Rewrite the beginning of these answers a) to c) for the students, using Student 1's answer as a model.

Student 1 is answering the question 'Explore the role of the artilleryman in the novel as a whole.'

And thinking about starting with…

Stop! You haven't got to write everything you know about *The War of the Worlds* in this exam. Focus on the question.

A better start is…

The narrator of 'The War of the Worlds' has two encounters with the character known as the artilleryman, whose main role is to express certain ideas about the world which are different to the narrator's.

a) Student 2 is answering the question 'How effective do you find the beginning and end of the novel?'

And thinking about starting with…

Stop! You are wasting time and words. Never begin an essay with 'In this essay I am going to…' Just get on with the answer.

A better start is…

b) Student 3 is answering the question 'Write about the ways Wells uses nature in the novel.'

And thinking about starting with…

> H.G. Wells, the author of 'The War of the Worlds', was a scientist, a Victorian and a teacher. He was born in 1866 and wrote a selection of books that have earned him the nickname 'the father of science fiction…'

Stop! Only a small amount of this contextual information is relevant, and anyway, references to context should be made as you go along as part of your analysis of the text. Make sure your first paragraph starts to actually answer the question.

A better start is…

----

c) Student 4 is answering the question 'Explain the significance of three different minor characters in the novel.'

And thinking about starting with…

> 'The War of the Worlds' is the story of an alien invasion. We know the earth has survived the attack because the narrator tells us at the beginning that the events he is describing happened 'six years ago'.

Stop! You are retelling the story. Use your first sentence to make a clear case for the three characters you are going to choose.

A better start is…

Exam requirements

Exams vary, as do the tasks you have to do on set books. Knowing the text as well as possible is the best way to get ready for whatever challenges you will face, but you should also find out as much as you can about the way in which you are going to be tested.

Activity 4

Carry out some research to find out the answers to the questions below. You can do this by:

- asking your teachers
- studying examples of relevant exam papers or past questions
- looking at the website of the exam board that runs your exam

a) How much time in total will you have read the text and get ready?

b) How long will you have to write your answer on *The War of the Worlds*?

c) Will you have to answer an open essay-style question or a question based on an extract from the novel?

d) Will you be allowed to have a copy of the novel with you when you are writing?

e) How many marks are available for the question on *The War of the Worlds* and what percentage of the total marks is this?

However you are being tested, you need to show that you have:

- an understanding of the themes and ideas of the novel
- an insight into and perception of less obvious meanings
- an ability to choose relevant evidence and apt quotations to back up points
- an appreciation of Wells's techniques and their effect on the reader
- a clear and fluent way of writing about your ideas
- a good vocabulary, and accurate spelling, grammar and punctuation.

Activity 5

a) Put the items from the list above into the following chart, ranking them from 'most challenging' (10) to 'least challenging' (0). Your finished list may not be the same as anyone else's because everyone has their own strengths and weaknesses.

Exam requirements	Level of challenge for me
	10
	0

b) Focus on the two things that you ranked the highest level of challenge and therefore feel least confident about. Write two action points for each. These should be things you can do before the exam to improve your confidence.

For example, if you feel that 'understanding the themes and ideas of the novel' is a weakness for you, you could decide to:

i. work through the 'Themes' chapter of this book again

and

ii. make a revision card for each main theme, including an explanation in your own words and three key quotations.

Close reading skills

Remember that, whatever the question, showing off your close reading skills is
your best chance of doing well. This means you need to:

- remember the main plot events and how they relate to each other
- consider how characters change and develop during the novel
- pay attention to the author's language choices and their effect
- link plot, characters and language to themes and ideas.

Activity 6

Practise bringing all your reading skills and understanding together by reading the
extract below from the beginning of Book 1, Chapter 3 and answering the questions
on pages 84–85.

Annotate the extract to help you answer the questions.

I found a little crowd of perhaps twenty people surrounding the huge hole in which the cylinder lay. I have already described the appearance of that colossal bulk, embedded in the ground. The turf and gravel about it seemed charred as if by a sudden explosion. No doubt its impact had caused a flash of fire. Henderson and Ogilvy were not there. I think they perceived that nothing was to be done for the present, and had gone away to breakfast at Henderson's house.

There were four or five boys sitting on the edge of the pit, with their feet dangling, and amusing themselves – until I stopped them – by throwing stones at the giant mass. After I had spoken to them about it, they began playing at 'touch' in and out of the group of bystanders.

Among these were a couple of cyclists, a jobbing gardener I employed sometimes, a girl carrying a baby, Gregg the butcher and his little boy, and two or three loafers and golf caddies who were accustomed to hang about the railway station. There was very little talking. Few of the common people in England had anything but the vaguest astronomical ideas in those days. Most of them were staring quietly at the big table-like end of the cylinder, which was still as Ogilvy and Henderson had left it. I fancy the popular expectation of a heap of charred corpses was disappointed at this inanimate bulk. Some went away while I was there, and other people came. I clambered into the pit and fancied I heard a faint movement under my feet. The top had certainly ceased to rotate.

It was only when I got thus close to it that the strangeness of this object was at all evident to me. At the first glance it was really no more exciting than an overturned carriage or a tree blown across the road. Not so much so, indeed. It looked like a rusty gas-float half buried, more than anything else in the world. It required a certain amount of scientific education to perceive that the grey scale of the thing was no common oxide, that the yellowish-white metal that gleamed in the crack between the lid and the cylinder had an unfamiliar hue. 'Extra-terrestrial' had no meaning for most of the onlookers.

At that time it was quite clear in my own mind that the thing had come from the planet Mars, but I judged it improbable that it contained any living creature. I thought the unscrewing might be automatic. In spite of Ogilvy, I still believed that there were men in Mars. My mind ran fancifully on the possibilities of its containing manuscript, on the difficulties in translation that might arise, whether we should find coins and models in it, and so forth. Yet it was a little too large for assurance on this idea. I felt an impatience to see it opened. About eleven, as nothing seemed happening, I walked back, full of such thoughts, to my home in Maybury. But I found it difficult to get to work upon my abstract investigations.

a) 'A flash of fire'; 'a heap of charred corpses'; 'improbable that it contained any living creature'; 'an impatience to see it opened': How do these references in the passage foreshadow future events?

b) Find three phrases that show the narrator's attitude to 'the common people in England' and explain your choices.

c) Using the text to support your answer, explain the narrator's attitude to Ogilvy and Henderson.

d) What views about science are conveyed in this extract? Use evidence from the text to support your points.

e) How do you think Wells wants the reader to feel about the narrator at this point? Refer to at least two different parts of the extract in your response.

Planning

Here are three essay questions that refer to the extract on pages 83 and 84.

a) Using this extract and two other relevant moments in the novel, explain how Wells presents humankind in *The War of the Worlds*.

b) Explore how Wells presents attitudes to science in this extract and elsewhere in the novel.

c) 'The narrator has an air of arrogance and superiority that spoils the book.' How far do you agree with this comment?

Activity 7

Using the ideas you came up with in Activity 6, and any other relevant ideas you have about the text, complete the following flow-chart-style plan for question a) above.

Opening paragraph – state that Wells presents a range of attitudes to humankind through the narrator's viewpoint. This depends on people's education, class and behaviour. Give two contrasting examples such as the narrator's attitude to Ogilvy (e.g. in this passage) and his brother's account of the masses leaving London.

Comment on the narrator's attitudes to people, using a range of examples – the narrator's neighbour who gives him strawberries, the boys playing in this passage, the man whose back gets broken, the kind family who look after him at the end.

Conclude by summing up positive and negatives about human beings, from the narrator himself to minor characters. End on quotation about humanity learning from the experience of the Martian invasion, which seems hopeful but realistic: 'Now we see further.'

Activity 8

Now practise other planning approaches. Choose either question b) or c) from the questions on the previous page and create a spider diagram essay plan or a two-column paragraph plan to show how you would respond in the exam. Whichever planning approach you opt for, aim for five main well-developed points and a concluding paragraph.

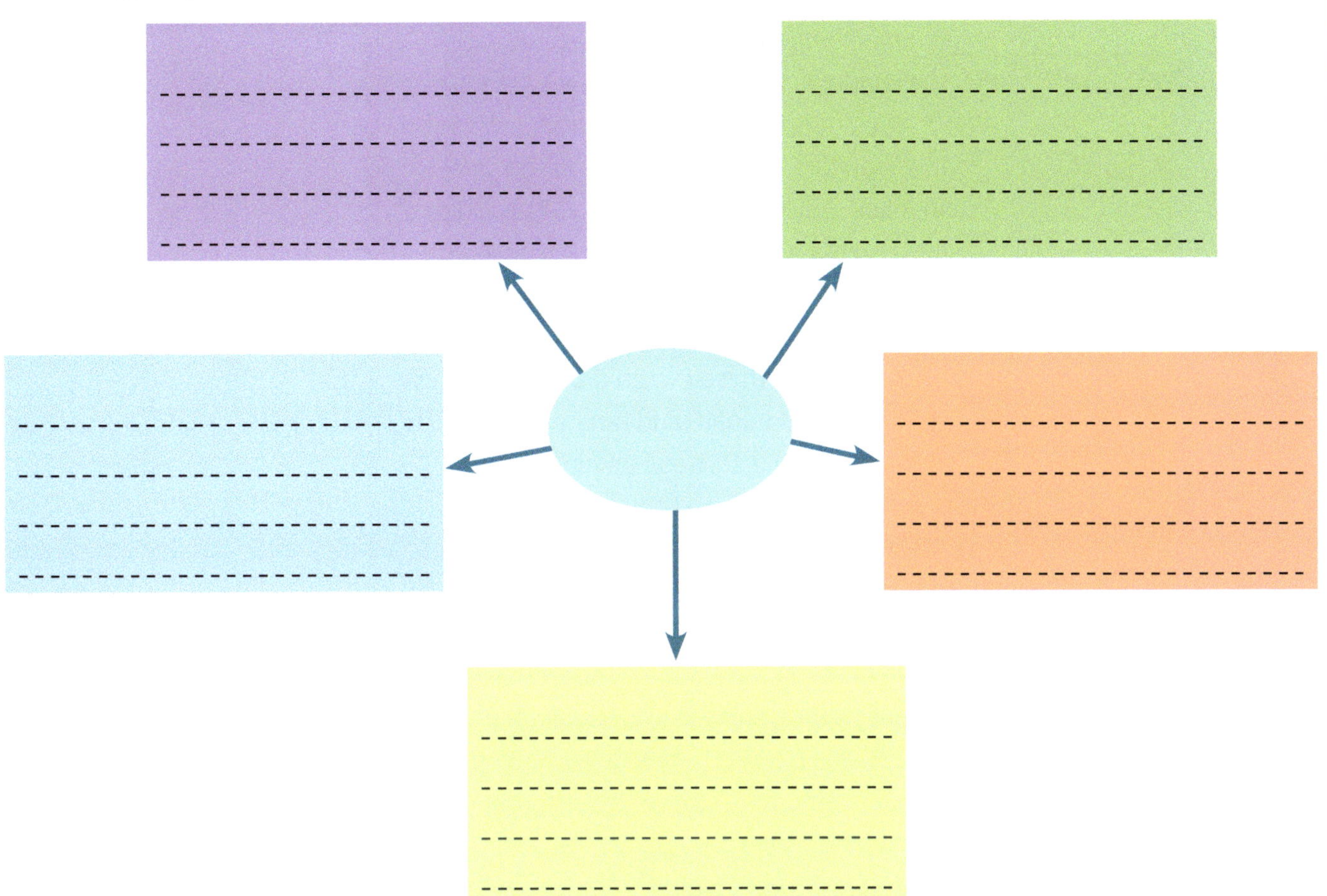

Main paragraph topic	Detail and quotations

Activity 9

Read the following source text and the example questions a) to c) on page 90. Circle the question you would answer and complete the plan to show how you would answer it.

Annotate the extract to help with your planning.

London about me gazed at me spectrally. The windows in the white houses were like the eye sockets of skulls. About me my imagination found a thousand noiseless enemies moving. Terror seized me, a horror of my temerity. In front of me the road became pitchy black as though it was tarred, and I saw a contorted shape lying across the pathway. I could not bring myself to go on. I turned down St. John's Wood Road, and ran headlong from this unendurable stillness towards Kilburn. I hid from the night and the silence, until long after midnight, in a cabmen's shelter in Harrow Road. But before the dawn my courage returned, and while the stars were still in the sky I turned once more towards Regent's Park. I missed my way among the streets, and presently saw down a long avenue, in the half-light of the early dawn, the curve of Primrose Hill. On the summit, towering up to the fading stars, was a third Martian, erect and motionless like the others.

An insane resolve possessed me. I would die and end it. And I would save myself even the trouble of killing myself. I marched on recklessly towards this Titan, and then, as I drew nearer and the light grew, I saw that a multitude of black birds was circling and clustering about the hood. At that my heart gave a bound, and I began running along the road.

I hurried through the red weed that choked St. Edmund's Terrace (I waded breast-high across a torrent of water that was rushing down from the waterworks towards the Albert Road), and emerged upon the grass before the rising of the sun. Great mounds had been heaped about the crest of the hill, making a huge redoubt of it – it was the final and largest place the Martians had made – and from behind these heaps there rose a thin smoke against the sky. Against the skyline an eager dog ran and disappeared. The thought that had flashed into my mind grew real, grew credible. I felt no fear, only a wild, trembling exultation, as I ran up the hill towards the motionless monster. Out of the hood hung lank shreds of brown, at which the hungry birds pecked and tore.

In another moment I had scrambled up the earthen rampart and stood upon its crest, and the interior of the redoubt was below me. A mighty space it was, with gigantic machines here and there within it, huge mounds of material and strange shelter places. And scattered about it, some in their overturned war-machines, some in the now rigid handling-machines, and a dozen of them stark and silent and laid in a row, were the Martians – *dead!* – slain by the putrefactive and disease bacteria against which their systems were unprepared; slain as the red weed was being slain; slain, after all man's devices had failed, by the humblest things that God, in his wisdom, has put upon this earth.

(*Book 2, Chapter 8*)

a) How does H.G. Wells use the features of horror writing in this extract and elsewhere in the novel?

b) To what extent is this a significant moment in the novel?

c) 'London about me gazed at me spectrally.' Explain the importance of place and geography in the novel as a whole.

After circling your chosen question, use the boxes below to help plan your answer.

Opening paragraph

-
-
-

Paragraph 2	Paragraph 3	Paragraph 4	Paragraph 5
• • •	• • •	• • •	• • •

Concluding paragraph

-
-
-

Practice

 **Activity 10**

a) This student chose question b). Read the answer below, then match the strengths of the piece on the top of page 92 (1–4) to the starred points in the answer. Write the numbers in the boxes.

> To what extent is this a significant moment in the novel?

This is a very significant moment in the novel because it is about the death of the Martians. After all the fear, tension and horror that has been built up, the narrator finally sees that the alien invaders are 'slain'.

Throughout the story, the narrator put in references to real places, just as he did in this passage. This creates a sense of reality in the novel, from the beginning when the Martians land on Horsell Common, to the brother's journey away from London, to these final stages of the narrator's journey.

It is interesting that the narrator sees the first dead Martian on a heap of earth on top of the 'curve of Primrose Hill' in the 'half-light of the early dawn' because dawn is a time of day that is a symbol of hope and new beginnings. Wells chooses language which reminds us that this moment is like the end of the war – when the narrator climbs up to the top of the 'earthen rampart' it is like he is reaching the place of the final battle.*

Another reason why this is a significant moment is because of the narrator's feelings. After a short time of being curios, for a lot of the novel he has been scared. Even at the beginning of this section the descriptions are like a horror film: 'the eye sockets of skulls' gaze at the narrator and there is a 'contorted shape' on the ground. Then he decides to be killed, and 'marched on recklessly towards this Titan'. The language at this point emphasis the theme of war. But at the end of this section the narrator says 'I felt no fear.' This isn't the end of the novel and he has still got to get fully over his experiences, but Wells seems to be showing the reader a bit of hope at this point.

Wells also uses the animals in the passage to show its significance. The birds that peck round the Martian give the narrator the first clue that it is dead. Then 'an eager dog' runs across the scene. All the way through the novel animals are used as symbols compared to humans. The birds and the dog are behaving in a new and different way, and now even bacteria – 'the humblest things' – are standing up against the Martians.

At the end of the passage there is a really long sentence. It starts with the conjunction 'And', which gives it a powerful and conclusive tone. Then it builds up with phrases describing the Martians. Then there is the world 'dead' in dashes which seperates it out from the text and makes it seem extreamly important. Finally, this sentence ends with four repetitions of the word 'slain', really emphasizing the narrator's amazement that the Martians have finally been defeated. *

So to sum up, this is a very significant moment.

Annotations for strengths

1 Strong example of language analysis using some correct terminology.

2 Effective reference to wider themes of the novel.

3 Excellent awareness of Wells's authorial intentions.

4 Paragraph openers help to make the answer clear and cohesive.

b) Now read the improvements suggested by the marker and make the corrections required.

Annotations for improvements

1 An abrupt ending that makes it seem as if the writer ran out of time.

Rewrite the ending so that it is more developed and thoughtful.

2 Some informal language and spelling errors that will lose the writer some marks.

Find all the informal language and spelling errors and write the correct form.

3 Paragraph 2 isn't relevant because no link has been made to the question.

Rewrite paragraph 2, linking the geographical specificity of the novel to the references in the passage and explaining why it helps to make this passage seem significant.

Activity 11

Write your own practice answer to one of the questions below on separate paper.
Use the table to check that you have included all the features of a successful answer.

a) In what ways is *The War of the Worlds* a successful science-fiction story?

b) Explain the importance of fear in the novel.

Successful answers show...	Tick or cross	Example from your own practice answer for each aspect
Understanding of the themes and ideas of the novel		
Insight and perception about less obvious meanings		
Ability to choose relevant evidence and apt quotations to back up points		
Appreciation of Wells's techniques and their effect on the reader		
A clear and fluent way of writing about ideas		
Good vocabulary, accurate spelling, grammar and punctuation		

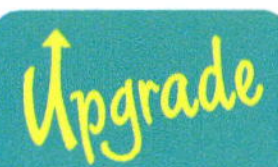

In any exam response, make sure you use key words from the question all the way through your answer and make sure each paragraph focuses on the question.

 # Progress check

Use the chart below to review the skills you have developed in this chapter. For each column, start at the bottom box and work your way up towards the highest level in the top box. Tick the box to show you have achieved that level.

I can sustain a critical response to *The War of the Worlds* and plan thorough, thoughtful and accurately written exam answers accordingly ☐

I can use well-integrated textual references from *The War of the Worlds* to support my interpretation ☐

I can use a wide range of vocabulary and can spell and punctuate consistently and accurately ☐

I can develop a coherent response to *The War of the Worlds* and plan full exam answers accordingly ☐

I can use quotations and other textual references from *The War of the Worlds* to support my explanation ☐

I can use a range of vocabulary and can spell and punctuate mostly accurately ☐

I can make some comments on *The War of the Worlds* and plan exam answers accordingly ☐

I can make references to some details from *The War of the Worlds* ☐

I can use a simple range of vocabulary and spell and punctuate with some accuracy ☐

Personal response

Textual references

Technical accuracy

allusion   a reference made to something without naming it

antagonist   character opposing and challenging the protagonist

apocalyptic   referring to the end of the world

chronological   in the order in which events occur

context   the circumstances that form the background to a piece of literature and can help readers to understand it

device   a technique intended to produce a particular effect or fulfil a purpose in a literary work

fictional autobiography   a fictional narrative written as though it is a true life story from a first-person point of view

fin de siècle   a French term (meaning 'end of the century') associated with the way that art and culture reflected changes happening at the end of the 19th century

first person   telling a story from the point of view of a narrating character, using the pronoun 'I'

foreshadowing   when an author gives clues, warnings and indications about future events

genre   a style or category of art, music, or literature

imagery   the use of visual or other vivid language to convey ideas and emotions

Industrial Revolution   the introduction of machinery into Britain in the late 18th and early 19th centuries. The period was characterized by the use of steam power, the growth of factories, and the mass production of manufactured goods

journalistic   in the style of a journal, with a detached, observational tone, focusing on facts and events

natural selection   Charles Darwin's theory that weaker and less able creatures die out over time, leaving stronger, more able species to survive

overcoming the monster tale   one of the plot types identified by Christopher Booker in his book *The Seven Basic Plots*, in which he explains his theory that all stories match one of seven plots with predictable features and character types

pathetic fallacy   a literary technique that gives human qualities or emotions to natural events, such as the weather, to reflect a particular mood

plot   the main events of a play, novel, film, or similar work, presented by the writer as an interrelated sequence

protagonist   the main character in a work of fiction

retrospective   looking back on events and situations

science fiction   fiction based on imagined future scientific or technological advances and major social or environmental changes, frequently portraying space or time travel and life on other planets

scientific romance   a tale combining science and mysterious or imaginary elements

serial   a story or play appearing in regular instalments, for example in a magazine. In Victorian times, this was a popular way of publishing stories in a more affordable format at a time when few could afford to buy books

setting   the physical and geographical backdrop of a play, novel, film, or similar work

socialist   a political view that property, business and possessions should be owned and run by the community for everyone's benefit

structure   the way a text develops across its parts

symbol   when something or someone represents something else, such as an idea

theme   a subject or idea that is repeated or developed in a literary work

third person   using 'he', 'she', 'it', etc. to tell a story from another person's point of view

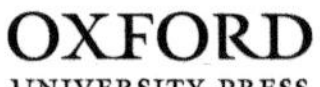

Great Clarendon Street, Oxford, OX2 6DP, United Kingdom

Oxford University Press is a department of the University of Oxford.
It furthers the University's objective of excellence in research, scholarship,
and education by publishing worldwide. Oxford is a registered trade mark
of Oxford University Press in the UK and in certain other countries

© Oxford University Press 2017

The moral rights of the author have been asserted.

First published in 2017

British Library Cataloguing in Publication Data

Data available

ISBN 978-0-19-841947-1

10 9 8 7 6 5 4 3 2 1

Printed in Great Britain by CPI Group (UK) Ltd., Croydon CR0 4YY

Acknowledgements

The publisher and author would like to thank the following for
permission to use photographs and other copyright material:

Cover: © MasPix/Alamy Stock Photo.